D0285277

They Left Their Tracks

Recollections of 60 Years as a
Bob Marshall Wilderness Outfitter

By Howard Copenhaver

They Left Their Tracks

Recollections of 60 Years as a Bob Marshall Wilderness Outfitter

By Howard Copenhaver

Copyright 1990 by Howard Copenhaver

ISBN 0912299-45-2 (Hardcover)
ISBN 0912299-46-0 (Softcover)

DEDICATION

To my family and to all my friends that lent me the encouragement that kept me going 'til I got the job done.

All Rights Reserved

No part of this publication may be reproduced, stored in a retrieval system, photocopied, or transmitted in any form or by any means without the prior written permission of the copyright owner or the publisher.

STONEYDALE PRESS PUBLISHING COMPANY
205 Main Street — Drawer B
Stevensville, Montana 59870
Phone: 406-777-2729

TABLE OF CONTENTS

Cover Photo: Howard Copenhaver, the dean of wilderness outfitters in Montana, is atop a high ridge in the Bob Marshall Wilderness, the scene of most of the stories in this book. Photo courtesy Diana Eck.

INTRODUCTION

You know stories are what makes people do things and want to do things. They build a desire in the old human soul to do something better and more spectacular than the experience they have read or heard about. You take all the true stories and fiction, but also the teller or writer has to enjoy a good story himself to be able to hold his listeners or readers. So what happens? Everyone builds in a bit of plain old bull that increases the interest of the reader or listener. The thing you have to do is learn to be able to sort out the bull from the unchawed grass and you will come up with the real meat of the sandwich or the truth of the story.

As the saying goes, "Truth is stranger than fiction" stands the test of time and is more true in the hunting world than any place I know. I have had the pleasure of outfitting for the sportsman from all corners of the world for more than 60 years. I call them the "Golden Years of My Life." What an experience to be personally acquainted with some of the greatest men of our great universe. I always say they are the greatest men in America and possibly in the world. Now I'll tell you why. First off, they are not an egotistical group of wealthy men who have a desire to just shoot and kill such as many try to make them out. They are men of the same stripe that landed on Plymouth Rock or traipsed across the Great Plains in search of something. They did not really know what they were searching for but they did know that they were not finding it in the life they were leading.

They are courteous, kind men and women of extreme feelings for the country, game and fellowman. In all my many clients I found only one man who hunted just to kill. I later found out he was a gangster stiff-arm gunman in the great days of law and disorder in Chicago.

Many are men you may not personally like but if you are psycho enough to go along with them you will find that golden quality that has inspired all of us at some time. Mebby I should say it's like painting a house. Some painters use a brush and some a spray gun, but they are both painters. I have found the basic quality of sportsmanship and desire that has made them a top doctor, lawyer or businessman in their hometown has put them in the field hunting—the desire to accomplish something that few in our many thousands of people of the world just plainly do not have guts enough to try. If they were not tops in their chosen field at home, they would not be in the mountains hunting a trophy because hunting is not for free and people without ambition rarely can pick up the tab for anything.

The sportsman's dollar has done more for game in the world than you can ever express in dollar signs. His generosity has helped build wilderness all over our North American Continent. I, for one, praise them in their undying efforts and want to thank them from the bottom of my heart for the opportunity they have given me just to know and be allowed to share with them the experiences and country, game and friendship they have given me.

I am going to jot down some of these experiences as they come to mind. In whole they will be true happenings—some funny, some serious, but as I said in the start if you find what you think is bull, well go ahead and feel that way. It's your pleasure. I'll try not to build it up too high and tell it as it was. Hope you enjoy it.

Three generations of Copenhavers—Howard, grandson Todd at left, and son Steve.

ADVICE

Well here I am again in a mess. If it wasn't for my friend Mike Korn, most people wouldn't know what I was talking about. I've wrote the stories and now I must tell you what I'm talking about. I believe you call it getting the wagon hitched in front of the horse.

What is outfitting? Well, outfitting is one of the oldest occupations in the western United States. It's how the West was settled.

The mountain men of old were outfitters. They used horses and mules to ride and pack their belongings wherever they chose to go.

Lewis and Clark were outfitters in making their journey across the West until running out of groceries forced them to eat up their transportation in the form of horse and mule steak. I believe they ate their last horse somewhere up on the head of the Bitterroot River in Montana or the head of the Lochsa River in Idaho.

The old wagon train masters were outfitters. They guided and saw to the furnishing of all needed supplies including groceries, water, most of the stock, wagons and wagon repairs, etc., for the trip across the plains from St. Joe, Missouri, to all parts of the West. No small task.

Later Buffalo Bill and many other mountain men outfitted wealthy English, French and German sportsmen in search of bison, elk, grizzly bear and our pronghorn antelope, all of them using horses and mules to ride and pack supplies on. This business has continued to the present day. In Montana, I believe, outfitted recreation is the second largest industry in the state.

The first pack saddle was called a sawbuck because it resembled a sawbuck used to hold wood logs while a man sawed blocks off. It was made of wood in an A shape that fit straddle of a horse's back. It was secured to the pack animal with cinches or belly bands that were fastened to the tree of the saddle. Diamond hitches were used to tie the gear on to the saddle and pack animal. Panniers made of heavy canvas bound with leather were used to carry the cargo, just like a apple box, hung on the saddle and loose gear such as bedrolls was placed on top and then covered with a six by seven foot tarp and lashed down tight with either a single or double diamond hitch.

Along about 1930 a fellow in Idaho invented a saddle he called a decker. It was a more humane and easier to use saddle. Two mantle (pronounced manti) covers are used for each animal. A mantle is a piece of heavy canvas, usually seven by eight feet. Your gear is balanced by weight and folded up tight in the tarp and tied solid with a mantle rope. A pack is slung on each side of your pack animal with a sling rope and secured. This lets your pack swing back and forth on your pack animal while allowing the blood to circulate through his back and keep it cool. With a sawbuck and diamond hitch, the load is cinched tight to the pack animal's back.

Now why am I trying to describe the pack saddle and how to use it when my good friends Smoke Elser and Joe Back have published whole books on it?

When an outfitter books a party for a trip into the mountains, he must pack enough supplies to last the full time. This is quite a trick. First you figure out the amount of groceries needed for one man for each meal and then multiply by the number of guests and crew. Then you add enough to last you for two days extra so, in case of an emergency, you have food. There are no supermarkets around the bend.

When you head for the hills, you have in mind a planned itinerary of where you will camp each night. Now in picking a camp location you must be sure to have available wood (dead trees), water, ample timber to protect you from wind and storm and last but most important, plenty of grass for your stock. They have to eat too. All this can usually be found in one place. I always try to select a very scenic spot, which is not hard in this beautiful wilderness.

Scapegoat Mountain in the Scapegoat Wilderness.

MY FIRST ELK HUNT

DATE: 1928. Along in October my father and two neighboring ranchers decided just what they needed was a full-fledged trip to the mountains. We really needed the meat for our winter grocery supply. You see, we only had several hundred cows and steers out in the pasture and 1,500 head of sheep eating their heads off. We had to have a winter supply of meat in the ole smoke house!

The years have rolled by and I have figured out what Dad and Old Ezra really needed was to take their old friend Adolph, who really knew the country, and get away from Ma and the kids. This was fine but Ma in both families says, "OK but you take number one and two sons with you." And that they did.

Boy! What a deal! We'd hunt deer and the mighty bull elk, fish in the creek and no school for two weeks. Huckleberry Finn never had it so good. We were to camp and hunt the Meadow Creek country right under Ole Red Mountain, the highest peak in our area. This country is the headwaters of the North Fork of the Blackfoot River.

Meadow Creek is a wide valley surrounded by high rugged ridges and peaks of over 10,000 feet with a beautiful creek and meadows forming the valley floor. From our ranch you could look high up to the east and there she was, a great pile of red rocks and cliffs. I had daydreams and night dreams of me and that mountain for years. Now we were going up there! What a thrill and unforgettable pleasure for a 14-year-old lad. I'll never forget it though I live to be a hundred.

At last the horses were shod, the groceries packed, tents and bedding loaded on the pack horses and away we went.

The climb to the divide was very steep, rocky and narrow trail. Lots of time we followed game trails as back then there were no good, well-maintained trails anywhere. If the party before you got through, you knew you could.

At last we gained the top and could look down into the Meadow Creek Valley. What a sight with Ole Red Mountain right smack in front of me!

Some of the glory went out fast as we started down the other side. Right off, the trail narrowed up with cliffs above as high as you could look and on the other side a sheer drop off of maybe 200 feet. We walked and led our horses and rolled rocks out of the trail. When they went over the

Red Mountain.

edge there would be no sound, then after a bit a great crash as they hit the bottom and crashed though the timber below.

Finally, we got to Alpine Park, the head of the valley. No artist could paint this on canvas. It is still beautiful, a grassy meadow surrounded by tall alpine fir trees and sheltered by the high rocky peaks above. Three or four miles below we came out of the timber into another such opening only much larger. It was here we were to make our camp. Wood, water and lots of grass for our horses, a must in any campsite.

Soon the horses were unpacked and turned out to graze. The tent was up and before I could really set down and devour the beauty of my mountain and valley it is getting dark and Pop hollers, "Come and get it 'fore I throw it out."

My enthusiasm was short-lived. Supper over the first night: "You boys do the dishes," "You boys get some wood," "Hey, the water bucket's empty." Now, it still wasn't that bad, but it sure ruffled a young hunter's mane to do those chores.

Next day, up the side of Bugle Mountain me and Dad go. I'm about like a colt on the first day of June with the bright sun on his back. Every few steps the Old Man (that's what us boys always called him) would stop and whisper, "Now if you see one just don't say a word, just level down fine and get him." Then away we'd go, always up. I'm rarin' to go and Pop's having a little trouble with weight, age and altitude. Then a pause and whisper, "Don't say a word, just level and shoot."

We approached the top of the ridge. We were topping out on a flat bench where we hoped the elk would be waiting. As Dad stepped up, I, from below, could look right between his long legs and looking right back was a cow elk with much the same surprise that I must have showed. Quickly through my mind ran a well rehearsed phrase, "Don't say a word, just level and shoot." So up came Mr. .25-35. With the muzzle right between the Old Man's legs, Ker-Boom she goes! Up in the air goes Pop with a shout that still rings in my ears, "What the thunder!" (his favorite cuss words). I never knew he could jump that high. Didn't take him long to land and I guess you know who he landed on. I sure remember where he lit.

Now, when the sermon was ended and he'd calmed down he says, "What did you shoot?." I says, "Over there by that log, I think I hit an elk." We walked over and sure enough there she lay, shot right between the eyes. To me she was the greatest trophy ever to come out of the hills.

Never again did my Dad ever hunt with me. We went on many hunting trips together, but he'd say, "Which way you going?" I'd say and the Old Man would head out the other direction.

Now don't go away because there is more to this story. Remember this is my first hunt. Sure, I'd shot lots of grouse, ducks and squirrels but this was what hunting was all about. Real game!

I forgot to tell you that the night before we started on this trip, Ezra's brother-in-law Earl showed up at his ranch. He was from Canada and going to parts unknown. He had an 11-year-old boy who was his nephew along. Now when Old Ezra got up the next morning Earl was gone and Ezra had another boy on his hands. Well, Dad and him talked it over and decided that two of us boys could ride the same horse so now we had young Ted along with us. He had no bed, no rifle and his hunting clothes were bummed from us kids.

Well, I'd got my elk so no one wanted to have me tagging along and Ted needed my rifle. I tells Pop, "I'll take the .22 six-gun and hunt deer close to camp." OK. Away everyone goes, leaving me with the dirty dishes and a well-burned Dutch oven to clean. Pa could burn more stuff in a Dutch oven than any man I ever knew but the soft stuff on the inside was mighty tasty.

After the camp chores were done I takes this pea-shooter and a box of 50 shells and start up the mountain. I hunted for a buck but along late in the afternoon I shot a big dry doe. She looked at me and disgustedly walked off. I knew I'd hit her. Sure enough, I found blood. I was stuck to her trail now, just like mustard plaster. Just before dark, I came up on her in her bed and I administered the coup de grace.

Right down below me I could see the light burning in the camp where I was supposed to have supper ready. I dragged, rolled, pushed and pulled 'til I got her right down to the camp. Far from being a big shot or a hero, I caught "Old Billy Hell" for shooting a doe. Finally, Adolph came to my rescue. He says, "It's all right. We're allowed camp meat." Well, they left me alone after that.

Ted and me were the same age and disposition. We got along right famous. So it was decided we should hunt together the next day and see if we could get Ted an elk. Was I the big shot now! I knew how she was done. After all I was a seasoned hunter. I'd hunted two days!

Well, down the river we go headed for the Lost Pony Hills. About 11 o'clock we picked up this big elk track and after him we go. We caught up to him several times but Ted would get the buck fever and couldn't shoot. We had a council meeting and formed a plan. Next time we saw Mr. Elk, I was supposed to be the rifle man. Now if I got the elk, Ted would claim it and we'd be the only ones who knew the story.

We had just crossed the creek at Lost Pony and came out of the heavy spruce timber to a big park. Laying right in the middle of it is this huge elk, sound asleep. I drops to one knee, levels on him. I guess it didn't look right to me cause I lowered my gun and raised my back sight as high as she'd go, took another sighting on Mr. Elk and touched her off. You should have seen that elk leave Lost Pony. I overshot him so far I think I might of hit someone in Helena, 100 miles away.

To this day, every time a hunter gets a touch of the buck fever I tell him how it was with me and we both laugh and understand.

From dreams to this.

LODGEPOLE, MEN AND BEARS

When you are writing stuff on paper, you got to be sort of careful. They tell me if you write something about a guy and use his name, he can sue the tar out of you and gather for his all that is supposed to be yours. I'm going to tell you a yarn about a guy and use his name cause I know he ain't got the dough to sue me and he knows I ain't got nothin' he wants that ain't wore out, so here goes.

Gene is my brother. We operated hunting camps in partnership for many long years. He's one of the greatest little guys I have ever known, a great hunter and a great guy quick on action and long on guts.

Well, we had a group of eastern hunters camped in the Big Basin country of the South Fork of the Flathead, now known as the Bob Marshall Wilderness Area. He'd take two hunters out and I'd do the same. We'd come in at noon and each take two more in the afternoon. Game was plentiful and there were not many outfitters in the state at that time. The extra hunters that were left in camp either fished, played cards or hunted on their own right close to camp till their turn came up to be guided after elk.

One day we came in at noon to change hunters and one of the guests asked if he could have a word with us outside the tent. We figured he had some little gripe he wanted to air so out we go. Well, it seems like Joe and his buddy had had themselves a nice little morning hunt up Stadler Creek but on the way coming back to camp they had to cross the creek. Right where they decided to cross a sheer cutbank of clay, a strip of lodgepole timber about 10 inches in diameter was between them and the creek. Now lodgepole have no limbs until right at the top so you have a tall stick tree. Poor climbing. Joe says, "Let's sit down and slide down the bank," so they did. When they hit the bottom, lo and behold, right between them, sticking out of the bank, is a black bear's head. Joe says, "What shall we do?" His buddy says, "Go to camp." They did, but forgot their rifles laying by the den of Mrs. Black Bear.

Now Joe is inviting Gene and me to go along and retrieve their trusty firearms. Well, away we went right after lunch. When we arrived at the cutbank we looked across the creek and sure enough, there are two rifles and a bear head on the clay bank. Gene says, "Joe, here take my rifle and get that bear right between the eyes." So Joe takes a rest on a tree and lets go, Boom! Mrs. Bear's head disappears back in the hole. We go over there to have a look-see. Sure enough, down at the bottom of the hole is a bear head with a trickle of blood right between her eyes.

Gene, as I said, was one of these little guys long on guts and swift on action. He dropped down on his knees and says, "Let me down and when I get a hold of her head, two of you pull me out." Now every hunter in camp came to help with this deal, so we had plenty of manpower.

Gene slides down the hole head first, gets his holt and hollers "Pull." Slowly they pull him out of the bear den. When Mrs. Bear comes in sight, two more hunters grab aholt of her and pull her out. Now comes the payoff! Just as they drop mama bear on the ground about two feet behind her comes another bear's head. Someone hollers, "Grab your gun." What a scramble! Before they got untangled here comes another bear right behind him with his buddy a bit smaller squealing and looking for safety. Then right on his tail is another bear squalling and squealing, and looking for daylight and trees. All told, out came two yearlings and two

On Jumbo Mountain skinning a bear.

cubs in search of freedom. What a sight! Six hunters and four bear all looking for altitude and nothing but slick lodgepole pine. Two hunters were trying to climb the same tree. One cub had it figured the same but being late to his chosen tree he went right up the back of poor Joe who seemed to be helping his buddy reach a limb. When the bear came to him, he did the same as he did with Joe—used him for a stepping stone. Needless to say, it was the greatest bear hunt, or man hunt, of all time, mass confusion with four bears winning the race for the top of the trees.

Joe and his buddy got their rifles. Joe had a nice bear rug and a few scratches on the back of his neck and head to prove he didn't get the last one.

Honey-bucket bear.

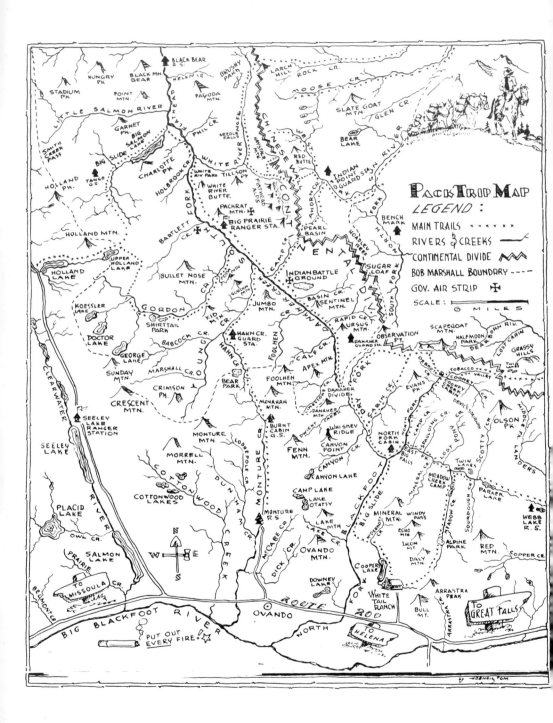

SMOKE AND COOKING

A pleasant and successful packtrip, be it for the outfitter or his guests, hinges heavily upon the crew you have put together—packers, horse wranglers, guides and cook. To me the cook plays a big role. It's like the Old Lady says, "A man with a full belly is a happy man." A camp cook does not have a lot of conveniences at hand. He makes do with a few pots and pans. Of course, today we have gas ovens and gas grills making it a lot nicer and easier.

Old Smoke, who you'll come upon in a number of stories, was a true Dutch oven and Sibley stove artist if there ever was one. He carried a roll of sourdough in the top of his flour sack and could make sourdough bread and biscuits that would melt in your mouth.

A Sibley stove was like a funnel. It was made of bright silvery tin. You would set it upside down on the ground and build a fire in it. When you had a big bunch of red coals in it, you would hang reflectors on the outside in holes spaced around and up the side of the stove to get different degrees of heat. They were bright tin plates with a floor wide enough to place your bread pans or meat skillets around the outside between the stove and reflectors. By learning to govern your heat with the damper and draft holes, it worked beautifully. Old Smoke could really handle this outfit—pies, cakes or what-have-you. Now, a cook is just like a carpenter. He has to have good lumber if he's to build a good house. Furnishing top quality groceries and meat is the outfitter's part of the deal, but I'm getting way off from my tale that I started so I better get back on the trail.

Smoke was an old roundup cook and he worked for us for a good number of years. One hunting season we were camping in the Old Danaher Ranch cabin on the head of Willow Creek in the South Fork country. It was 28 miles by trail from the ranch. We would make the trip in one long day, but everybody planned on a tough day's trip back then. Smoke was getting up in years so he would stay in camp while we rode out and changed parties at the ranch.

We had been gone for three days and upon returning late the night of the fourth day we were not greeted by Old Smoke when we rode up in front of the cabin. No light in the window. Just a small wisp of smoke coming out the chimney. I went into the cabin and there was Smoke stretched out on his bunk belly down. I says, "What's the matter, you sick?"

The cook at work with clients lining up for chow.

He says, "I'm going to die. I fell and sat on a sharp rock three days ago and I can't stand the pain." No light statement by a vet of the Johnson County Sheep and Cattle War and more.

Our hunters were in the cabin by the time Gene had a light going. Now, this hunt we had a group of old army doctors. They were rough and tough. It had been a long, hard day and bitter cold. They had fortified themselves with plenty of Old John Barley Corn squeezins along the way. They were feeling no pain.

Doc Gil says to Smoke, "Unbutton your pants. Let's have a look." So with a gas light and flashlight he examines Smoke's tailbone. Now me and Gene we can see this big abscess about as big as an orange and bright red right where his tailbone should be.

Dr. Walter was a surgeon. He says, "Give me your hunting knife." Someone did. He walked over to the stove and stuck the blade in the flames and over his shoulder says, "You guys lay him on the table belly down and hold him." While this was being done, he pours some whiskey over the knife and Smoke's butt and says, "Hang on."

He cut that abscess with that knife and you should have heard Smoke scream. Then he sort of relaxed on the table and kept saying, in a hoarse whisper, "Thanks Doc. Thanks Doc." Well, Doc got his little black bag after we had unpacked the duffle, cleaned and sterilized the incision with antibiotics and Smoke was back in business again.

What had happened was he'd went out hunting, slipped and sat on a sharp rock, bruising his tailbone. Infection set in and he had an abscess. The hunt went well from there on, but Smoke never left camp until the season was over and we packed camp out of the hills. He healed up and rode the 28 mile trip home without a hitch.

TRY A TEPEE SOMETIME

When we were just kids going to school, my Dad and a number of his friends, all ranchers in the area, would set up a hunting camp each fall over the mountain in Meadow Creek right under Red Mountain. Usually this happened about the 15th of October.

Now us boys weren't too smart at that time so Mom insisted on us going to school. We were going to high school in Missoula. We'd drive an old Model T Ford the 75 miles and it would take us at least four hours one way with bum roads and flat tires. Now on Friday night right after school, Gene and me would take off for the ranch and hike into camp. It was only 12 miles straight up and straight down. We were tough. We'd hunt Saturday and Sunday and then hike home Sunday night and go back to school Monday morning. Now you can see we had to love hunting and the mountains.

The main thing I learned early on is to put up a good camp first thing. Well, on this one trip Old Ezra and George talked the rest of the crowd into leaving all the tents home—too much to pack in and out. Ezra says, "We got a big tepee from some Indians and they taught us how to work the wind chute. We can really run this outfit like as if we invented it." Now running the wind scoops on a tepee is an art you don't just take one lesson on a calm day and master the job. The Indians had many years of experience and an inherited trait that was bred in you as a child.

This particular trip it was a beautiful October night with about six inches of new snow, a bright moon and stars you felt like you could reach up and grab a handful of them. We made the pass along about midnight. Looking down from up there on top of the pass was spectacular, with my friend Old Red Mountain jutting high in the moonlit sky. We dropped down to Dead Man's Lake in the head of the valley and were really making time down the trail when, Bam!, we ran into a herd of elk coming up the trail to meet us. I don't know who was more surprised and spooked, us or the elk. No thought of shooting. Anyway, what are you going to do with an elk when you can't even see your gun let alone the sights.

When Gene and I got close to camp we couldn't see any light. The closer we got the more concerned we got. "Mebby they camped in a new place," I says. "No," Gene says, "I can smell smoke." Then we see this big tepee looming up out of the dark. Right around the bottom of the rig was a light line. It went up the side walls about one foot; then the tepee was dark. I says, "They've went to bed." We open the entrance flap and, boy, the smoke. All the hunters were flat on their bellies holding a skillet, coffee pot or something over this little fire in the middle of the tepee.

What a mess! If you laid on the ground you had about eight inches of clear air to breathe and see through. Now you should have tried to sleep in that smokehouse. It was about 3 o'clock in the morning when we crawled in there. We did our best to sleep until daylight and get some breakfast. We ended up building a campfire outside and making some coffee and broiling some ham on willow sticks.

We knew we did not want another night of this so off we go to hunt over the mountain and down to the ranch that evening. The only animal we saw was Old Boots, our dog, when we walked up to the house and she ran around us sniffing and snuffing like we were two Virginia smoked hams. I think those old boys missed part of the lessons the Indians tried to give them.

One of our "back when" hunting camps.

TRAP MOUNTAIN BULL

We were camped this year on Basin Creek in the Big Basin country of the upper South Fork, a spectacular basin about three miles wide and five or six miles long with beautiful meadows on the river bottoms and craggy limestone peaks on all sides. Willow Creek came down a narrow gorge from the Danaher where it opened out into this basin then on the northwest end entered another canyon and headed on down to Big Prairie on the main river.

We had a party of hunters from Des Moines, Iowa. The weather wouldn't give us no help at all. It was bright and sunny all day with the temperature in the 60's and as high as 80 degrees. Consequently, no snow. The main elk rut was over.

Now you know with this kind of weather you just have to find that certain little spot where a bull elk is hiding out putting on some fat. These spots are usually near a slide or little open meadow with lots of heavy brush and black timber to hide in. I have found bulls holed up like this lots of times. They'll find a spot where there is water, lots of soft feed and dense cover to hide in. They'll park right there for days at a time and you can walk right by them within 50 yards and they'll never move unless you see their tracks and goose them out.

I had this fellow, Carl, I was guiding and we were right near the top of Trap Mountain. We could look for about three or four miles down and across this big ampitheater basin. It had several large snow slides coming down into it with heavy strip timber on the ridges between these slides. A beautiful piece of elk country. Just what those old mossy horns like.

When I speak of snow slides I am not talking about a strip of snow down the mountainside. We speak of snowslides being barren strips down from the high mountains left because the snow sliding down in winter has swept the trees off, leaving long, open areas from the top to the bottom of the mountain. New shrubs and grasses grow lush on these slides producing some of the elk's most desired food.

I said, "Carl, let's set down here in this snow slide and eat our lunch and glass the area with our binoculars 'til it cools off a bit." He says, "Jake. I need a rest anyway."

We hadn't glassed very long when I spotted an old bull. He was bedded in a little depression in a snow slide right across the basin from us. I show-

Trap Mountain bull.

ed him to Carl and I said, "We'll have to go all the way around that basin to get to him. It's about a mile and a half around there, but if we truck right along we should get there about the time he starts to feed." Carl says, "I can hit him from here." I says, "That old .06 won't do it. You'll just goose him." He says, "Now look here. I was captain of the Des Moines Rifle Team and we won the Olympics three years ago." No argument. I believe it was the only time this had ever been done. He says, "I also won the gold as an individual." I still says, "No, let's slip around there. We can come out on that little timbered ridge right above him. Carl, it's kinda like an Old Indian once told me, 'If you shoot from here mebby you hit him. Then you have to go see. If you go first up close you know you kill him. You walk two ways anyhow.'" I won out and away we went.

After about three hours we slid out on this little hogsback and right below us was this depression, but no bull. Very disgusted, I sat down and started glassing again. Carl is really upset and telling me how he could have hit that bull. All of a sudden, I swing my binoculars over on the spot where we had eaten lunch. There's that cockeyed bull climbing right up the snow slide where we had been sitting. I says, "Carl come here." He did and I says, "Now it's no farther from here than it was from over there to here. Let me see you do your thing."

Carl pulled an army rangefinder out of his pack, sighted through it, turned a couple of screws and says, "Right at 1,100 yards." He jacked up that old military sight, took a good rest over a log using his coat for a sand-bag and turned one loose. I was watching through my glasses and saw a puff of dust just below the bull. The bull gave a big jump and stopped. I says, "Four feet low." He jacks up that sight again, takes his time and down come the bull. Now if I had not been there, I would not have believed it could be done with an old Springfield .06. Mebby it was over 1,000 yards or shorter, but I know from experience it was over 800 yards.

It was dark as the inside of a cow when we reached that spot again. I found where we had eaten lunch. Carl says, "How we going to find him? It's too dark." I say, "We're close because I can smell him. Let's build a big bonfire and mebby we can find him." I started a fire, gathered a bunch of dead fir boughs and said, "I'll step down the hill a piece and when I'm ready you throw the fir boughs on the fire. They will flare up and give me some light." Carl threw the boughs on the fire and being so dry they really flared up bright. There laid our bull not 50 feet down the slide. We dressed him out and caped him by bonfire light and headed for camp five miles down the mountain. When we got to camp Gene says, "What you guys trying to do, burn that mountain down"?

Was he a good shot or lucky? I say this man could shoot.

Scapegoat Mountain.

A nice six-pointer.

FAT MAN AND A BEAR

It seems like many years ago. Must have been somewhere in the early Thirties. I had a group of fishermen in on a trip. We were camped at the Youngs Creek crossing on Cayuse Prairie in the South Fork of the Flathead, a beautiful place to camp and wonderful fly water.

Youngs Creek is really a river. It flows to the northeast right off of Leota Peak and Pyramid Mountain. She comes roaring down a steep, grassy valley, runs right into the cliffs of Jumbo Mountain and down to the main South Fork River. One of the most beautiful streams in the hills with big spruce and tamarack and cottonwood trees along its banks. It can only be appreciated by those fortunate enough to see it with their own eyes.

One evening along came two friends of mine, Ting and Babe Wilhelm. They were outfitters from over on the Swan River. They were packing for a group of geologists from an eastern university. The group was a walking group consisting of professors and students.

One professor was a huge man, not so tall as just huge in symmetrical proportions. He looked like a 50-gallon gas drum with legs, arms and a head on it. It is hard to conceive probably, but he actually walked with one foot in the trail and the other up on the bank. It was really hard for him to negotiate mountain trails.

Well, Babe rode into our camp and after a greeting asked if we minded their camping next to us all night. We said we'd be glad to have them so they pulled over across the park and camped about 100 yards away.

Now on these summer trips no one ever packed a tent, just a fly or two in case of rain so everyone bedded down to suit his or her fancy. The fat guy, I'll call him Big Foot, grabbed his sleeping bag and walked out into the middle of the park and spread it out. It was beautiful weather with a moon that all lovers wish for. Now if you haven't seen a Montana moon in full, you just can't realize how bright it can be.

We'd all got to sleep in fine shape when a series of the most blood curdling screams came from the middle of this park. We sat up and looked out there. There, half out of his bag was the white form of Mr. Big Foot and kind of setting back on its haunches was a big black bear. The bear gathered himself up and left straight east, Big Foot straight west. Ting took his wrangle horse and headed up the trail after Big Foot but could not persuade him to come back to camp. He hiked the 33 miles out that night and by noon the next day. Neither Ting nor Babe ever heard of him again.

Now what really happened must have been something like this. We'd been camped there for four or five days and this old camp bear would come around and the guests would throw him an apple or orange or sometimes a candy bar. He was harmless and tame. From the position of the bear and Mr. Big Foot, I am sure that Mr. Bear in search of a handout had walked up and smelled Mr. Big Foot right in the face. I can only guess what both Mr. Big Foot and Mr. Bear thought when Big Foot opened his eyes and screamed.

A string of horses in the Big Basin.

HUNCHES

All of my life I have believed in what people call hunches. To me they are something else. I firmly believe if God wants you to get an elk, deer or whatever, you'll do it. If He doesn't, you're out of luck.

I have had so many hunches pay off with dividends. Old Dutch, who cooked for me for many years, used to say, "If Howard and his hunters leave camp and head off a different direction than he'd planned on, they'll come back with a bull." Sometimes I'd get up in the morning planning to hunt a certain area and on the way I'd get a feeling like as if someone was pulling on my arm to turn me off course. I always follow these feelings and usually they'd pay off.

To show you what I mean, not over four years ago I was helping my son, Steve, by doing the cooking. His hunting party showed up with two extra hunters. We had to have another guide, a two-on-one deal. He asked if I felt like guiding that trip and his wife, Donna, would cook. I decided to try it again even if my legs didn't work too good.

The night before the first day's hunt I had this sort of a dream. Me and the hunters came over a rocky ridge above a long plateau, sort of a meadow, and looking down I saw 14 cows and calves bedded down, plus a bull. After I got up the next morning, I kept trying to think, "Where are those elk and that meadow?" All of a sudden I knew, so off the three of us went riding our horses. We tied them up and took off on foot for the lodgepole benches on top of Whiskey Ridge.

We were about up to the top of the ridge when the wind changed. Now I knew if we topped out, the wind would be at our back and spoil our chance if I was thinking right. We dropped down and around the top to the north side of the ridge, climbed up and through a rock cut in the cliff. It was as steep as a cow's face. Peeking over the top, there they were. Just perfect. Seventy-five yards away were 14 cows and calves bedded down, plus three bulls; two were spikes and one a big heavy-boned six point. The spikes were between us and the cows.

I says, "There they are. Take that big bull at the bottom on the left." My boys started shooting. They each killed a spike. The old herd bull trotted across the meadow over the hill and never had a shot fired at him. Did the hunch pay off or was I just a lucky fool?

Another time the camp was full on elk except one gentleman who in three hunts had seen no bull and only a cow or two.

I started out for Dwight Creek this morning as I knew there were elk there somewhere. We got up the creek to where we were going to leave the horses. Now all the way, somehow I couldn't get the idea out of my head that I was wrong and should go to Lake Mountain about six miles from where I was—in the opposite direction. All of a sudden I say to my man, "I've changed my mind. I've got to go to Lake Mountain. I know our bull is there." He said, "You're the guide." We turned around and went to Lake Mountain. As we passed camp everybody was hollering, "You guys lost?"

We tied our horses and took up this game trail. We had gone mebby 30 minutes and right in front of us, grazing in a little meadow, stood this big six-point bull. After a bit of pointing I showed him to my hunter. One shot and he had his bull.

Does a man need help from up above? I say "yes" even if you call it a hunch.

Spring Creek bull.

WOMEN ON THE HILL

Years ago hunters, that is your average guest, wanted elk, moose or deer for the meat. Not many were concerned about Boone and Crockett heads. I've left far better elk and mule deer heads laying on the mountain than I've seen packed out in many years. Now, the reason is simple. Our hunters wanted good steak. Few cared about them Baloney Bulls, poor steak. They were more satisfied with a two-year-old dry cow or a calf, both good eating.

We had a party, usually of 14 to 16 hunters, who hunted with us for a number of years in the 1930's. This was a man and wife deal. Back then who shot what didn't seem to matter that much as long as everyone in camp had a hunting license.

With this particular party the men would hunt until they filled their licenses. Usually they wanted a young bull or any bull. Their wives hung around camp, went fishing or riding someplace. They just didn't seem to care for this hunting bit. Oh, once in a while one of them would get with it and hunt.

Well, this year I have in mind we had seven men and their wives. We talked to them before we left the ranch. "We are through packing out elk for you that your husbands have shot. From now on you shoot your own or nobody shoots." This was agreed upon before the start of the hunt.

One pair of these hunters were Peg and Jim. Jim was head pilot for TWA Airlines at that time; the other men were pilots under Jim. Peg was his wife, a beautiful dark-haired little woman with fire and brimstone shining from her eyes at all times, and it was her birthday coming up on a day on the trip.

Before leaving the ranch Jim presented her with a handmade 270 rifle with silver and gold engraving with her name on the stock, which was made of Mother of Pearl imbedded in the wood. She was tickled pink but would not carry it in a rifle scabbard on her saddle for fear of scratching it or getting sweat off the horse on it. Gene and I wrapped it up in some blankets and canvas and packed it on Old Blaze. Old Blaze was a very good saddle horse we were taking for an extra.

Well, all went well until the second day on the trip, about four miles from camp. We were going along a cutbank trail above Willow Creek just about to break out into the open meadows of the basin. Guess what? Old

Donna Copenhaver with beauty all around.

Blaze stubbed her toe and over the bank she went, head over heels. What a crash when she stopped in the creek right on top of Peg's new rifle! We got Old Blaze back on the trail and down to the meadow before we unpacked him to look at the gun.

You talk about a funeral parade, we had it. That beautiful stock was so broke up in small pieces it wasn't any good for starting a fire. The rest of the gun shined in the sun as good as new. Peg was crying and Jim promising a new stock when he got home. It didn't help. For several days all anyone had to do was say "gun" and poor Peg would start to cry.

When we got to camp, as usual, all the men and guides went after bulls. There was lots of game in those days and not many hunters. I guess in about five or six days the men all had their elk. Some of them were going after mule deer and a couple wanted bear. Anyway, at supper this night I turned to this gal, Peg, and says, "Are you going hunting elk with me tomorrow?" She says, "Sure, I'll go. I'd like to get one with one shot just to show that Jim man of mine I can do it." Just like that, the excitement of the hunt hit the rest of those gals.

Now, before bedtime it looked like I'd have a harem tagging along next day. I tried to talk some of the other boys into taking some of them. But, no, all these gals wanted to hunt together in one big group. Boy, am I in a mess! After much coaxing, Old Adolph agreed he'd go along. "Now, I'm going to ride in the rear," he says. "I don't want that bunch of females with guns behind me."

Well, next morning we loaded up on our saddle horses. Amid good-natured ribbing of seven husbands, we left camp. I'd had a hunch the night before that I'd better head for Foolhen Creek where there was a lot of open slides and a big burn to glass. I knew if we could spot a bunch of elk feeding early that morning and I could ride close enough and get some of these gals just to shoot, even if they couldn't hit them, I'd have made my day.

As you ride up Foolhen Creek on the horse trail you follow the creek in a tight canyon. Then you come to a ridge you have to climb. This ridge makes a hook off to the right up and around and joins Jumbo Mountain. This is where the big 1918 burn starts. No trees, just a few snags and stumps. I know the country like the inside of my sleeping bag. Just over the hogback and down below along the creek was a meadow about 300 yards long and mebby 100 yards wide. Up to the south went the steep side of Alloy Mountain. As I started up the trail into the burn, I heard a bull bugle. I stopped. Then another bull turned loose giving it all he had, that high-pitched whistle long and clear, ending with a series of grunts. One was on my right just over the ridge, the other to my left a bit but straight ahead, both right over this hogback ridge.

I jumped all these gals off their horses, got their rifles, and Adolph and I tied up the horses. Well, we lined these gals up in a line. He took one end and I the other. We explained the situation and all walked up to the edge of the ridge just like Cox's army. Looking down into this meadow, we saw that it was covered with elk feeding this way and that. I says, "Pick your elk and shoot at the same one. If you hit it stop." What a volley! When we saw seven elk down, Adolph and me stopped them.

I says to Peg right beside me, "Which one did you get?" Peg says, "I didn't shoot. I don't know anything about this gun." Quickly I showed her how to shoot and said, "See that cow and calf going up that snowslide?" They were about 250 yards up, the cow in front and calf right behind. There was peep sights on the rifle. I says, "Look right through that hole, line that gold bead up on the cow's neck and let her have it." She sticks this rifle up in the right direction. I'll bet it was waving around in a foot circle. Ker-Boom! Peg shoots and down the hill rolls the calf.

Old Adolph says, "What a mess. Guess we might as well start butchering." "We'll help," says the girls. So down the hill we go. They were laughing, crying and singing. We showed them the art of field dressing an elk on the first one and they did the others. Away they went at it, two or three gals to an elk. They'd jab a knife in and rip guts, hide, hair and all. This was a real mess now. Finally the job was done and we were back to the horses.

Adolph and I were washing our hands in the creek when here comes one of the gals with a jug to toast the hunt. They wouldn't wash their hands. They rubbed blood on their faces and their clothes were already a mess. Off to camp we went. By this time the jug was empty but the gals weren't. Old Adolph and me brought up the rear of this female war party. Everybody in camp could hear us for 30 minutes before we arrived. Needless to say, when their husbands heard the story the party really put on a new edge.

The next day the whole camp went to help pack out the girls' game. We led fourteen pack horses into this meadow, loaded a elk quarter on each side and away we went down the trail, the meat string headed for the home ranch.

What a hunt! There'll never be another like it in my time. They were the greatest bunch of gals that ever grew hair on their heads. I surely wish I could see them again.

Howard and Marg Copenhaver, late in the summer of 1962.

ARMY

Back about 1939 or 40 I had a party of fishermen from Houston, Texas, going into White River and they wanted to also fish Big Salmon Lake.

When they arrived there was only five of them. I asked where the sixth one was and they said he'd be in on the plane four days later. He was held up on business somehow.

Now, I had this problem as it would take us two days to reach White River and then I'd have to come back after this guy and return to White River. I could make it out alright in one day, but it was 58 miles to White River from the ranch and it was too much of a ride for a guest going back into camp. So I told them I'd be gone from camp for three days at least. They said, "That's all right. We'll just fish the South Fork and White River from camp and Jimmy, the cook, said he could take care of all the rest."

So I left camp about 5 o'clock in the morning and rode fast, trotting and loping my horse when I could, and arrived at the ranch about 10 o'clock that night. Someone from the ranch had picked Army off the airways and he was waiting at the ranch. While I was eating supper, I told him how far to camp and that it would take us two days to get there.

He says, "Those dirty sons ----- told me we'd be at a lodge and never said anything about riding a horse." He says, "Can you ride it in one day?"

I says, "Sure. I did today. I left camp this morning but I just had myself and a saddle horse."

He says, "If you can do it so can I."

I told him, "If you'll do it, I'll make it."

Now Army is about 6 foot 1 inch and thin, very slim. No extra fat anyplace.

I said, "OK, Army, get to bed. We'll leave about 3 in the morning.

Next morning we were on the trail. I'd already taken his duffle and sleeping bag in on the first trip, so we had just two saddle horses and a little stuff he'd brought along in our saddle bags, along with a couple of sack lunches.

When we'd hit flat ground, I'd kick our horses into a trot and sometimes a lope. We stopped at the Old Danaher Ranch and ate a lunch. We were getting right down the pike. We'd made 28 miles so far. I rested our

Crossing the South Fork of the Flathead at White River.

horses and Army for 30 minutes or so and then mounted up and headed out again. Army really is surprising me, no bellyaching, just riding and telling me how he'll get even with five Texas bull artists.

Along about 4:00 or 4:30 we hit Big Prairie Ranger Station and had a cup of coffee or two. Army is showing wear. He says, "How far left?"

I says, "Just six miles. Can you make it?"

He says, "Hell, yes. Just give me an hour to lay down and I'll be ready."

Well, in an hour I woke him up and loaded up again. We rode about a quarter of a mile and came to the gate at the end of the airstrip. I got off and opened the gate. Army rode through and here the trail forked. He says, "Which way"?

I says, "Take the right hand fork."

As I shut the gate, Old Army let out a cowboy yell and drug the reins off of where the colt sucks and down the trail he goes on a run. I catch up after a bit and slowed him up. Those horses were tired.

When we dropped down off the White River Bench to cross the South Fork to camp, he says, "Now how far?"

I says, "Across the river and about a half mile down the bank.

Army says, "Let me rest for awhile."

It's about 6:30 in the evening now and we've got lots of time to make camp, so I took a snooze with him. About an hour or so later I awoke and got him up. I says, "I'm hungry. Let's see what the cook has for us."

He got on his horse sort of tender like and I took off on a trot. Those horses were anxious to get to camp. When Army sees the camp he lets out a yell and loped into camp, jumped off and says, "Where's my fish pole?" The other guys got his gear and he says, "Where's the best fishing at, up or down?"

They said, "Downriver."

Old Army took off downriver and went fishing. He didn't wait for supper and came back to camp way late and went to bed. Next morning he tells me, "I surely showed them guys. They think I was fishing. I just went around the bend and crawled under a tree and went to sleep."

The rest of the guests never knew that he wasn't fishing. All they could talk about was how tough he was and how surprised they were that he was so tough. I don't think Army ever told them to this day that he didn't know how tough he was either and I know I didn't.

While on this story, I will tell you one that happened while we were on this trip.

Well, one day we decided to go up to Salmon Lake and fish for bull trout. Bull trout are really Dolly Varden. They grow up to 25-30 pounds. The largest I've ever seen was 33 pounds. They start their spawning run about the first of September in our country. In late August they start getting ready for it and congregate by the hundreds. in large numbers at the inlet and outlet of Salmon Lake. They strike well at this time of the year. You use a Daredevil or large spoon, sometimes a Pike Minnow.

So we went up to the lake to give them a try. Now when we rode into the park at the upper end of the lake, we met two friends of mine, Babe and Ting Wilhelm, who were packing the camp for a group of "Chicago" schoolmarms who were hiking through the wilderness. We stopped to talk and pass the time of day, when one blonde-headed gal walks up to my horse and starts to ask me questions. She asked them so fast I thought she was some kind of government agent on a special survey of some kind. I couldn't get time to answer one question before she had three more. All of a sudden she saw I was packing a six-shooter on my belt. She says, "Why are you carrying a gun?"

I sees my chance and says, "Well I pack some walking parties like you guys sometimes and someone is always breaking their leg falling over logs or rocks, and I've had to shoot a few of them."

She says, "You're lying."

I say, "I am not. If you pack someone with a broken leg on a horse and he smells blood it ruins him and horses are expensive."

She come back, "You're a liar."

I says, "No. There's a blue sky law in Montana that says you must not let a guest suffer, so we just shoot them."

She says, "If that's true, why doesn't Ting (her packer) carry a gun?"

I says, "He does. Just you ask him." Now Old Ting had been listening and when she walked over to where he sat on his horse, he never even waited for her to ask him about his gun. He just reached into his saddlebag and pulled out this old hog-leg, showed it to her and stuck it back

Howard and Army with bull trout taken the summer of 1941, the largest a 20-pounder.

in the saddle pocket.

We parted and went our ways. Now Ting and his party were going on a circle trip around the China Wall and back out this way on the return. Now it all went well with our fishing and I for one forgot about this gal.

When we were packing out, heading back to the ranch, I was leading the string in front and I came around a sharp turn in the trail right in a thicket of second growth trees. Right in front of me stood two of the schoolmarms and laying on the ground in the trail with her head on a log was this dumb blonde. I stopped my horse and jerked out my gun and said, "I'm sorry, but I have to do it."

Well, she let a scream out of her and took off through the brush on her hands and knees. Me and these other gals started laughing and I rode on up the trail. All of a sudden, she started yelling at me and cussing me like a teamster mad at his mules. I hope she didn't teach those Chicago kids the things she called me.

Later that year I saw Ting and Babe, his dad. As soon as they saw me they started laughing and told me about this gal. Well, it seemed Ting and the rest of the party entered into the game and kept cautioning this gal about getting hurt and had told her my job was to enforce this law of the Blue Sky Color. They had her so goosered that when they'd come to a narrow trail she would crawl on her hands and knees.

Also, they said she was still cussing me when she left for home.

A HELPFUL HAND

You know game wardens are a breed of their own. Everyone is their friend until hunting season opens; then they have no friends, so's to speak.

Well, a warden friend of mine was coming down the road on the first day of hunting season when he was frantically flagged down by two women. They showed him a doe deer all dressed out right beside the highway. They were really shook up seeing it was illegal to kill does.

Their excited explanation was that they had come upon two hunters loading it into a pickup truck. Evidently, they had given the two men a piece of their minds and they claimed the men had taken up the road and left the deer. One woman said it was a blue Chevy with a No. 5 license on it.

Lewis and Clark county is No. 5 and the Chevy was likely headed for Helena. Mr. Game Warden took after the pickup, calling ahead to the highway patrol to stop said vehicle. After 25 miles down the road and no pickup, the game warden called off the chase and returned to pick up the deer but, lo, no women and no deer—just nothing but some blood and guts on the road.

He told me this himself and I'm sure the two ladies are still laughing far louder than we were.

Steve Copenhaver with a bull trout.

A HONEYMOON ON HORSEBACK

You know when you ask someone about their honeymoon, they really come alive. They'll tell you about the great time they had in Vegas, or how tall the buildings are in New York, we climbed the Statue of Liberty, it was so much fun in Frisco, the wind blew every day in Chicago or you've just got to see Honolulu sometime. Not me and my little gal. We just start laughing and tell of a honeymoon on horseback.

This goes away back to the days of World War II and before. This old boy, not so old at that time, was very much in love with a beautiful gal. She's still beautiful today, a little bit gray on the sides but very well kept. The big question in my mind was "Should we get married now or watch this war thing?" Well, as it happened, "Bang," I joined the Navy in '41 and that set the stage for a long time to come.

While I was home on leave in '44 we tied the knot and were all set for a honeymoon. Only thing was, Uncle Sam says, "Not now, we still have things to do." It was off to sea again.

After the battle of Leyte Gulf I ended up in some hospitals and finally am stateside and have a convalescent leave coming. Me and the little lady says, "Here's our chance." I says, "We'll go home and take a honeymoon trip through the South Fork. I'll show you the Great China Wall, we'll fish the White River and the main South Fork. You'll love it, Honey, just the two of us and our horses."

Now to get to the China Wall we had to travel three days up the North Fork of the Blackfoot River and then the Dry Fork of the North Fork, crossing the Danaher Pass and down through the Danaher Valley to the Big Basin. The North Fork and Dry Fork is a narrow valley following the river all the way, a scenic, open fir tree country with high mountains on each side, very nice going and extremely beautiful. When you cross the divide the Danaher Valley widens out along Willow Creek with wide and long meadows for nine miles. High mountains surround it. You have Danaher, Apex, Foolhen and Toura Mountain on the west side. On the east is Concord, Scapegoat, Sugar Loaf and Investus, all high peaks looming up above the timberline. They are of white limestone with the bright green meadows and heavy timber to timberline. It is beautifully spectacular with a meandering stream down the middle of the valley.

Old Tom Danaher homesteaded in this valley in 1901, built a ranch house, barn and outbuildings that are gone now. His only access to civilization was by packstring and the venture was uneconomical. Due to this and health problems, old Tom had to give it up.

Now the dream of every good sailor is a diet of ham and eggs. It seems as though people who eat 50 pounds of beans every day can't see anything else. As you'll find out later, this ain't good.

We arrive home at the ranch expecting to take right off. No such luck. Horses are not shod, equipment not ready. Guess I just expected too much. Well, we got our groceries, duffle and gear ready, but no horseshoes, so I convinced myself they'd do all right barefooted as it was spring of the year and the ground was soft.

Finally, away we go, each with a saddle horse and me pulling two pack horses when I should have had three. Now I had been in hospitals for four or five months and not ridden since 1941. I was weak, soft and not in too good a shape. Poor Marg had been riding an office chair for at least seven years and never had she experienced a trip like this.

We made it to the Old Danaher Ranch the first day—28 miles. Not much of a ride; I'd ridden it before many times. Well, I'll tell you what. If we could of crawled into our sleeping bags without unpacking those horses I'd have done it. I finally got them unloaded and turned out to graze, set up a sort of a camp. Marg was cooking, pooped and crying. I'll tell you something. I'd a cried with her but I didn't have enough steam left to do it. However, after finding a jug in the duffle and a round or two of coffee royals and ham and eggs, the world looked brighter. We went to sleep to the tune of horse bells and a babbling stream nearby. What a tranquilizer!

Then comes the rude awakening, getting up and moving. We had sore muscles you can't believe. Even the top of my head was sore. We laid over here and recuperated all day.

Next day, bright and sunny, we rode to Camp Creek. Now we'd have some of that fishing. I love to fish and Marg can't wait to cook and eat some. The water was high, this being early in June. I couldn't get any fish to come look-see. Not one strike. You know on the other side of the fence the grass is always greener. Well, I says, "Let's get our horses and cross over to that side of the river where a clear stream is running into the main river. I know the fish will be laying right in the edge of that clear water."

We got our horses and forded across to a point, tied them to a tree and went to fishing. Time flew by and so did the sunshine. Along came the wind and rain. Marg says, "Honey, I'm awful cold."

Well, now the fish are biting. It's been four and a half years since I was fly fishing and I lose what little Sir Walter Raleigh manners I had and say, "Well, get on your horse and go to camp."

The fish are still biting when I hear Marg's voice, rather high pitched, talking to Old Blaze. I look up and her and Blaze are faced with a three-foot cutbank at the edge of the river. Before I can give directions to turn upriver to where the trail come in, Old Blaze gives a big jump and the bank gives away and what a hell of a splash. Marg underneath, Blaze on top. Well, Blaze bounds out of the river and heads for camp. Now, Marg's hat is lost in this scuffle, so down the river goes Marg after her hat. She is running and falling in about three feet of water. The hat is making time now. Marg is holding her fish pole high above her head as if she don't want it to get wet. In the end she loses the race. We never see the hat again. Now me, I can only see this from the funny side and I'm laughing my head off. Marg climbs out of the river, mad as a wet hen and screaming and I guess you know Blaze and me have had it.

Now Blaze can munch grass all night, but me, I have to get into that tent for something to eat; also, my dry clothes, sleeping bag and dear wife are in that tent. I know you've all heard about the Man Without a Country. Well he had nothing on me except I had plenty of wet country and no tent.

Well, I took my time taking care of our horses and walked up to the tent as sympathetic as can be, but every time I got close I'd see something more funny about it and giggle. Then the valley would ring with this unforgiving, screaming voice. I'd back off and give her time and then take another chance. Now I thought I'd seen mad women. Yes, I've had my hands and face slapped a few times, but I never realized a woman could talk so loud and fast when she was mad. I'll tell you she was mean. Right now I don't recall how I made it into the tent. I think she finally saw something funny about it too cause we ended up eating together and woke up to a nice day next morning.

After breakfast we go after our horses. Whether the yelling, laughing or both caused it, or if they were just lonesome I don't know. We found them 10 miles back along the trail at Danaher. Me and Marg are in mighty poor shape so we decide to ride them back to camp bareback. Now I'll tell you I've had a blister or two before but none like Marg and me had the next day. They were big as a dollar. This slowed us up a mite in travel time the next day but we made the East Fork of the Sun River, right under the China Wall.

To get to the China Wall country from the Basin you have to go north and east up Camp Creek, a very steep and rocky trail climbing up to Pearl Basin. This is rugged country with sheer cliffs and very rocky trails. The only way to describe it is to say tough and spectacular. When we went over the pass we were traveling on from three to thirty feet of snow. It was hardpack and would hold the horses up. Dropping out of Pearl Basin into Ahorn Creek, we slid the stock down a big snowdrift to where the snow ended. We were now in the Sun River drainage.

We had clear sailing up the west fork of the Sun River to the China Wall. Now the China Wall is really the Lewis and Clark Overthrust. What happened here is that the west side of the mountains dropped down and the eastern exposure raised up, leaving a sheer rock cliff or wall along the whole east front of the Continental Divide for a span of some 50 miles. The highest of the cliffs are from 1,500 to 3,000 feet, weaving in and out along the divide. Big cirques or basins lay below with spruce and alpine fir clumps scattered throughout the grassy floor of the basin with huge, big rocks here and there and lots of little creeks and spring holes of water. Elk, mule deer and mountain goat along with the grizzly bear love this country. Sunrise on these cliffs is a magnificent sight to behold.

Now some old-timers had told me that you couldn't take a pack string south along the Wall and come out on Indian Creek at Molly Creek Pass. Well, we did but what a trip. Ended up in the awfullest downfall mess you ever saw and night dark as the inside of a cow. Now my lovely bride was right there with me all the way, almost as mad as she was at the river but not quite. She cooked supper while I set up camp. I was learning. If your wife will still cook when she's mad, you're still OK or she's awful hungry, one of the two.

Well the payoff was next morning. I see a Forest Service telephone wire about 100 feet from camp hanging between two trees. I crawl over a few downfalls and guess what! There was the Molly Creek trail. Sure would have slept better if I'd have seen it the night before. Now I still get the knife every once in a while about the Great White Hunter who got lost under the China Wall. All went well, beautiful in fact. We saw elk, deer, a wolverine, scarce in those days, and sneaked up on about 40 mountain goat in one bunch on the side of Haystack Mountain. Then we dropped down to Murphy Flat at the mouth of White River from Molly Creek Pass.

When you come through Molly Creek Pass the view is impossible to describe. You have to see it to believe it. As you come up into the Pass you can look north along the east side of the Wall and see red and white limestone cliffs with one basin after another stretching out below you to the north, bright green with silver strips of water meandering through them and down to the east ending up in the Mississippi River. I have gained this spot many times with parties that were laughing, talking and having a big time but when we come out in the open all is quiet, just like you turned off a switch—they just sit there and look. I'm sure the picture lives with them until they die.

When you ride over to the west side of the Pass you can look north along the backside of Haystack Mountain and up White River to Silver Tip, Spinx Mountain, Turtlehead and west to the main valley of the South Fork River and White River, see the silver water shining up through the timber and grassy meadows miles below you. White River comes out of a white limestone country. All of the rocks are white, like snow. This whole White River drainage was burned off in 1916, leaving a big spectacular open area. Thousands of acres, how much I don't know, just a lot of scenery.

Off far in the distance to the west you can see the tips of Tango, Holland Peak, Swan Peak and the Mission Range, all covered with glaciers, looming up behind.

Down White River we go to camp at the junction of the South Fork at Murphy's Flat. Murphy's Flat is a big benchland of meadows along the river dotted with majestic ponderosa pines. It was named after Joe Murphy, who was one of the early day outfitters in the Ovando area.

Layer after layer of mountains stretching into the vast distance is awe inspiring and humbling to the visitor, pointing out how insignificant man is in God's great universe.

Next day I was raring to catch some of those White River natives, but no. My lovely wife decides it's wash, shave and bath day. After much ado, I found a five-gallon oil can at Murphy's hunting camp and assured her if she just soaked the clothes in it all day they would rinse out much easier. Well, she mixed up a whole bunch of warm, soapy water in the can and stuffed all the dirty things in it and away we went fishing. What a masterful way to solve the problem!

Now we didn't have a good fly rod. I found two old ones at the ranch needing much repair. I taped them together and rigged us out as best I could. After all, all we were doing was fishing! I was a little easy on my pole when a fish hit, but Marg would hang that hook good and hard every time she hooked a good one. All would go well until the fish hit shallow water and really started to fight. Bang would go her pole in a new spot, sometimes two or three spots.

After a few hours of this and the sun on the water as well as the white rocks of White River it was too much. Now you remember she'd lost her hat. Well, by this time she had a suntan of brilliant red. None of these new fangled tan lights could duplicate it in 100 years. So off to camp we go with our fish.

When we arrived at camp, what a mess. All my darling's wash was scattered all over in the sandy riverside. Calmly standing by, chewing on the leg of a pair of long-johns was this nice old mule deer doe.

Well, we soon had the mess cleaned up and ready for supper. Fish? As I told you, every sailor wants ham and eggs. My ham and eggs and Marg's sunburn and broken fish pole just didn't set the stage for a pleasant honeymoon. We did real battle this time. I'm sure each of us realized we should not both lose our tempers at the same time after that.

Next morning we are visited again by our friend the mulie doe. What a mess! She was wasp-waisted, gaunt and talk about dirty. That soapy wash water sure did the trick.

By this time our barefooted horses were real tender. I gave Marg my horse. I rode the pack horse and dragged Old Blaze the last 40 miles to Hahn Cabin on Youngs Creek. This was to be our last day on the trail. We cut our trip short because of the sore-footed horses, but I'm sure if we'd have had a longer honeymoon, neither of us or the marriage could have stood it.

Now this sounds like Marg is mad all the time. Well, it ain't so even though I've given her plenty of reason to be. We have stuck together for 45 years and shared a great life of matrimonial bliss.

On this trip we really had a wonderful time. As I said, Marg had not seen any of this before. We saw several hundred head of cow elk with freshly born calves, and watched the cows hide their calves with one small chirp when they saw us. Then the cows disappeared as if by magic right before our eyes. Coming down Monture Creek on the Ovando side of the Divide, we bumped into a grizzly and watched him run up the mountainside for three quarters of a mile and over the ridge without even pausing for a breath of fresh air.

Then we had a nice visit with Old Horace Godfrey and his wife, who had arrived at Big Prairie Ranger Station the night before we arrived there. Horace was the Forest Service ranger for the Flathead District at that time. This developed into a long friendship.

By the time we got back to Seattle and the Navy, Marg's skin was replacing scabs and the blisters on my butt were healed. All in all, it was a great trip. We are thinking about another honeymoon but not on horseback. I only wish we were young enough to try it again.

A trophy he did not want. Howard and Clarence with a big grizzly.

A DISAPPOINTED HUNTER

There was another guide who worked for me for a number of years. He was just a plumb good hand anywhere, but he had one distressing quality. He was deathly afraid of a grizzly. He claimed he wasn't. He called it respect. Be it respect or fear, he wanted no part of them in any way.

He was guiding this tough luck hunter for elk. The hunter had hunted elk over much of the elk country in the Northwest for 15 years and had seen only one bull elk. In his words, "I saw one bull and stood there like a fool and watched him walk away."

Now Pat and the hunter were coming down along a creek late one afternoon when they came to a little meadow in the thick timber. Out in the middle is a big brown bump laying right in a spot of sunshine. The hunter says, "Is that a grizzly?"

"It sure as hell is," says Pat as he heads up a tree.

Now Mr. Hunter lays it to the bear with that old 7-magnum three times. Mr. Grizzly just sort of flattens out on the ground, never even kicked. The hunter inspects the bear, shot three times through the neck. Pat says, "To hell with that bear. Let's go to camp." And to camp they came. We finally talked Pat and the hunter into going back next day just to see if the bear was still there.

Well, our hunter had done a good job and after much decision-making they skinned out the bear and brought the hide to camp. This was by far the largest grizzly I have ever taken in all my years in the hills. Clarence, the hunter, was hunting elk and that "cotton-pickin" bear was a waste of time as far as he was concerned. We tried to convince him that he had a trophy that any hunter would take above all if he had the chance.

To me, and I'm sure all outfitters will agree, in North America the Number One trophy is either a Grizzly or Rocky Mountain Bighorn Sheep. Here is a hunter who has accomplished this and shows his disappointment any way you look at it. To him, the whole trip was a complete failure. He is old and rheumatic and this is probably his last hunt.

When we got to the ranch (still no bull), I knew I had to do something or his disappointment would do me no good when he talked to his friends at home. We loaded all the elk and deer meat and heads and capes in the pickup with the duffle. I put this grizzly bear hide on top. We were going to Missoula to the taxidermist and freezer plant and then to the airport. Now

Camp kitchen after a visit from a bear.

I made sure Clarence rode with me.

When we reached the outskirts of the city, I stopped and spread this bear hide out over the top of all the meat and duffle. It covered the whole pickup box and when I opened the tailgate the head hung to the ground. He was big! Then I drove slowly up the main drag and stopped right in front of the First National Bank. I says, "I'll be just a minute in here." When I came out there was such a crowd around that pickup I couldn't hardly get to it. Now, just as I'd hoped, right in the middle of them telling the story of how he got the bear was my hunter. Boy, was he steamed up and proud of that bear. I dropped off the hide at the taxidermist, gave instructions and made the airport on time.

A couple of months went by when we received this letter from the Old Boy's wife. She said, "Can't you get that taxidermist to ship that bear because if it is growing like Clarence's story, we'll have to build a new house when it arrives."

JUST CHARGE IT TO ME

I guess it is only human nature but I love a story told at someone else's expense. I really liked this story told to me by a Washington State game warden while I was at a sports show. He was complaining about the lack of satisfaction realized in his work. Also, he was really concerned about the lesson a convicted hunter learned and how much it controlled the do or do not do of an illegal hunter.

The story goes like this. It seems like the hunter is a real shooter with lots of time on his hands and money to burn, a very well-known sportsman who is in the habit of packing a roll of greenbacks around that would choke a hungry cow, a big tipper and free spender with many followers.

This happened late in the duck season. My game warden friend was after him just like a bloodhound; sworn to catching him dead to rights and dropping the hammer on him once and for all.

We'll call the game warden Bill. Well, Bill spots his poacher out on a lake with the northern flight of mallards just falling out of the sky into the only open water on the lake. The hunter is shooting ducks like mad, retrieving them, then another flock would come in and the process would begin all over again.

Bill knew where the hunter was staying in an old cabin a short ways from the lake. Now, Bill calls in some other game wardens and sets up a greeting for the hunter when he comes home that evening. Along about dark the hunter drives up to the cabin, steps out of his car and starts dragging ducks out of the car. On come the lights and he is surrounded by law personnel. The ducks are put in gunny sacks and Mr. Hunter is stowed in the local slammer that night.

Next morning both ducks and hunter are led into the judge's chambers. After Bill gives his explanation of what really happened, the honorable judge says, "Mr. Hunter, how many ducks do you have in those sacks?"

The hunter replies, "Sixty-four, your honor."

"Are you guilty?" asks the judge.

"Hell yes," says the hunter.

After a bit of deliberation the judge says, "This will cost you $1,800 cash."

Mr. Hunter says, "Fine," reaches in his pocket and pulls out a roll and peels off eighteen $100 bills to the judge's secretary. She writes him out a receipt.

Just as the hunter opens the door to leave, she hollers, "Sir, you've made a mistake. I owe you $100."

Says the hunter from the doorway, "That's OK, just put it on tomorrow's hunt."

Fisherman on the South Fork of the Flathead at Bartlett Creek.

LUCK OR KNOW-HOW

For many years, 19 in all, we outfitted a group of hunters each year. It became a sort of ritual that none of them cared to miss. They would renew old friendships and stories as well as have a few drinks and a game of cards to top out the hunt.

One of these fellows, Lee by first name, had made six or seven hunts—always coming out the same. No game. You could try as you wished but when you were guiding Lee it was no soap. Guess you'd just call him a hard luck hunter.

Like one day I had him and his buddy, Howard, up on Concord Mountain. We spotted a bunch of elk feeding in a high plateau, probably about 40 or 50 of them. Now you'd think Old Lee could hit one of these. We sneaked in close and was all ready to shoot when the wind shifted and left us high and dry with no elk, just tracks.

Well my brother, Gene, says that night, "I'm going to take Lee up Fiction Creek and we're not coming back till he gets a bull."

Fiction Creek comes down right off the west side of Sugar Loaf Mountain, a high spectacular peak forming part of the backbone of the Continental Divide. It is a deep, narrow canyon that was burned out in the big fire of 1918. New growth had come back in the thickets of jackpine along with some spots of old virgin fir, a beautiful bachelor pad for lonesome old bulls. One could climb up on one side above the new growth and glass snowslides and open burns, but it is steep, rocky and tough on man or beast. When you've hunted Fiction, you've earned your star.

Away they went. When they returned that afternoon, Lee is right up in the stars. Everyone knows he's finally killed his bull elk. But here's what really happened.

Gene spots this old six-point bull sound asleep in the middle of a snowslide. There is heavy timber along the near side and just a few jackpine up and down the middle of the slide. They slip up close and there he stands all ready to jump off the mountain. Gene says, "Let him have it fast." Lee bangs away and the bull disappears behind a jackpine. Out he bounds seeking solitude and "bang" goes Lee again; then the bull is behind some more trees. In another bound Mr. Elk is on his way for parts unknown. He has shifted into overdrive now and is running full speed. Lee takes a final shot as he disappears.

Very disgustedly Gene and Lee walk out on the slide to inspect tracks for a chance of blood. When they reach the first jackpine, there lays a six-point bull. Flabbergasted, they rush down to the second clump of pine. There's another six-point bull. When they came to the third clump a little below them stands the third bull. Gene administers the coup de grace and the butchering starts.

Lee hunted with us for a good number of years after that. His luck reverted back and he never fired a shot until the last year he hunted. By this time he was a man in his later seventies. He went home successful with a nice fat cow and claimed he had planned it so we could pack all his bulls out at one time and not waste a whole day each year.

At Moose Creek along the China Wall.

RELIGION ON THE MOUNTAIN

For many years I had the pleasure of outfitting a great dry fly fisherman and his party in the South Fork of the Flathead country every year. This fellow would always bring with him six or eight of his staff, one from each branch of his business. He was very well heeled and also extremely generous as he always furnished all liquor and picked up the tab for the whole shebang. They all flew out in the company jet.

B.F. had called me and asked if I could set him up on a short packtrip of five or six days where he could have a one day ride into top fly fishing. This is a tough bill to fill. A good fishing spot a short ways from the outside is tough to find.

I finally settled on packing in over Holland Lake Pass and down Salmon Creek to a spot just above Big Salmon Lake. We planned to take one day going into camp, staying there and fishing for three days and ride out on the fifth day. This would necessitate trucking equipment and stock 160 miles but I could do it and keep them happy.

Holland Lake Pass is extremely high and was a very rough trail back then. We arrived at camp and while we were setting up camp B.F. got his fly rod and went fishing. All the other guests were flaked out in the shade resting up from the ride.

When camp was set up, I took off down the creek to see how B.F. was doing. I was worried because Salmon Creek is narrow and swift with lots of brush along the bank, making it a difficult stream to fish. There were lots of cutthroat trout in the stream, mainly because fishermen don't like to fly fish with a brushy bank behind them. When I caught up I just stood and watched him throw that fly. He was an artist with a pole and dry fly. I could see he was far too good a fisherman for the water in this creek. Walking up to him I said, "B.F., we should set down on a rock and have a little talk."

He said, "Fine." So I told him how I felt about the stream and his ability and that I knew what kind of water he really wanted and if he would bear with me I'd move camp and give it to him."

Now this was in August. The weather was nice and warm with bright moonlight at night. I says, "If we have an early supper, pack up and move camp tonight, I can have you on the big river at the mouth of Little Salmon River in about three hours. The rest of your crew have been

Smoke's bridge.

resting and sleeping for two or three hours now. Also, it will be a spectacular ride in the evening and early moonlight."

He says, "OK, let's go."

As soon as supper was over I loaded them on their horses and sent the cook to guide them. The packer and I loaded the camp on the mules and took after them. Big Salmon Lake is a quarter to a mile wide and winds in and around Charlotte Peak for five miles. With the moonlight and shadows on the water it was gorgeous. From across the lake the cry of the loons and quacking of ducks backed up by the howling of a she coyote and her pups blended something into the ride I'll never forget. I still hear from Hal, who was on this trip, and he says the same.

Little Salmon is a stream mebby 50 to 100 feet wide and from six inches to two and a half feet deep. It rushes out of a canyon and drops into the main South Fork of the Flathead River, making a long, deep hole at the bend of the river. This water is as deep a blue green as the blue sky above.

When camp was set up and we had coffee boiling in the pot, Mr. B.F. walks up to me and says, "Howard, you are a smart, honest man. I could go home tomorrow and go right back to work and enjoy it. This was wonderful." (A compliment I treasure.)

One day he says to me while we were sitting on the bank of Little Salmon River enjoying the evening with a highball, "Howard, I have an

Going in the high country after them.

elderly gentleman from Sweden who has taken care of my yard, flowers and building for many, many years. He is around 70, very slim and wiry, an extremely hard worker. Now, I would like to do something for him beyond a yearly bonus at Christmas time. Do you think 70 is too old a man for you to take hunting? I know he has dreamed of hunting big game all his life in this country."

I said, "I would be glad to take him. A lot of men 70 can do more than younger men who are in ill shape physically."

Well, it ended up that George, I'll call him, came hunting with a party, six in all, from the plant. We left the ranch and packed into hunting camp. Early the next morning (it was Sunday) everyone was in a rush to get out hunting, but not George. He would not hunt on Sunday. I can see this and respect any man's belief.

So Monday morning George and I set out for Whiskey Ridge, which has produced many a good trophy. It is a rather gentle mountain with open sidehills and scattered, big fir timber and lots of water and many open parks. By 10 o'clock we had a real go-around with a couple of bull elk. They were really bugling good, raking the trees and grunting. George and I were on a cliffy sidehill, the bulls and their cows below in heavy timber.

Along about 10 a.m., as elk do, everything went quiet. We waited for a while and I said, "They're all asleep. Now let's move in closer and wait for the afternoon hunt. I believe they'll start bugling about 4 o'clock."

We hadn't gone 50 yards along a game trail that put us right out in the open when right above and behind me a bull let go a blast. We dropped to the ground and waited. Then I bugled an answer. He came back hot and heavy. I gave him another toot. Back he came. Then out from behind a tree not 70 yards away steps a big six-point bull and bugles. I says, "Take him low in front, George."

George ups and lets go. The bull stops, looks all around, then bugled again. This went on while George shoots nine times, never close to the bull. All the time the bull is moving down the ridge past and beyond us, bugling, then stopping to graze. At last he went behind some trees.

I grabbed George's arm and said, "Follow me," and we ran 50 yards downhill, coming out behind the trees screening the bull elk. I stopped and said, "Let him have it, George." By now we are only 50 yards from the bull. I think he can't miss. No shot. I say, "Shoot, George," all the time keeping my eyes on the bull. Then I hear something strange. I look around and George is unloading his rifle. I says, "What's the matter?"

George says in broken Swedish-English, "Howard, if God wanted me to kill that magnificent animal, I'd have hit him the first shot. But no. He let me see him and if that's the way He wants it, it's good by me. I'll go home and hunt rabbits and remember to thank Him for this privilege in all my prayers."

We watched the bull as he grazed down the sidehill, bugling as he went. He stopped just before he entered the timber and joined his harem; he stood with his nose in the air and bugled a long farewell.

George did go home without his bull and I'm sure he went back to hunting rabbits and with every one he shot at I'm sure he was looking at a grand six-point bull on a rocky ridge and offering a prayer of thanks for this God-given privilege of just sitting and watching a big bull in his own kingdom defying another to come take his harem of cows.

IT'S A HORSE

There probably is nothing an outfitter or guide loves to do better than pull a guy's leg, especially if the guest is gullible. Most people who are gullible seem to enjoy being the object of a joke. This young lad was 19 years old, a farm boy whose father had given him this hunting trip for a graduation present.

He was tall and slim, long, shaggy shoulder-length hair. He was as wild as a March hare and couldn't wait for us to get started for camp, getting in the way as we were packing the mules, trying to help. He sure was in a hurry to get the show on the road.

I for one kept ribbing him about his long hair and said I was going to cut it so's he could see where he was going. Dan and Steve also were having fun with him as well as the other guest watching the show. That night after supper, into the kitchen came this lad. He says, "Mr. Copenhaver."

"Nobody calls me 'Mister,' just 'Howard'," I says. "What can I do for you?"

He says, "You got a hair cutting scissors?"

I says, "Yes," and I sure gave him a haircut. I trimmed his foretop so's he could see.

Dan was guiding him. Now Dan liked him and was trying hard to show a good bull. He and Dan had covered a lot of rough ground in the last few days to no success. They'd had bulls bugling, seen cows, but no good bull. Dan says to me that night, "Where would you go tomorrow?".

I says, "Well nobody has been up the right hand fork of the Dry Fork yet. It ought to be good."

So Dan and the lad head that way. They had been climbing up a open ridge when they stopped for a sandwich. Dan give a squeal on his bugle and "Bingo," back comes an answer from up the ridge. Dan waits a bit and toots his horn again. Back come Mr. Bull with a long lonesome bugle. Dan knows now he has a lover looking for cows.

Dan bugles again. The answer comes back hot and the bull is coming down the ridge on the very trail they are setting on. Like a flash he hides himself and hunter behind an uprooted old tree, gets the kid all lined up with a rest and tells him not to move as the bull is coming down to them. Now he bugles a challenge again and the bull comes back hot and heavy but has stopped behind a fir thicket not 50 yards from them. They can see the saplings waving from the bull raking them with his antlers. He's really hot now and bellowing his head off. Dan is digging deep in his ditty bag of tricks to get him out of the thicket. Sometimes you can get in a spot like this and Mr. Bull will just shut up and sneak away.

Finally Dan gives a shrill squeal out of his bugle. Out of the thicket comes the bull. He has fir boughs hanging on his antlers and he's on a trot, headed right at them not over 30 yards now. Dan says, "Shoot."

The kid says, "Oh no you don't. I'm not going to shoot some guy's horse."

Dan is about as wild as the bull is and he says, "Shoot. Did you ever see a horse with horns on his head?"

The kid jumps up and screams, "You're right." The bull whirls, headed for parts unknown. "Bang" goes the kid's rifle and down goes the bull. He runs to the fallen elk, stands admiring him. Dan walks up and the kid looks at him, turns pale and screams, "Dan, I'm getting sick," and up come what's left of his breakfast.

Now this boy's license was still good for deer and black bear but, no, he had to go home. Steve says to me, "You need some fresh vegetables. Why don't you take him out?"

The next morning I left for the ranch. When I got there I loaded the kid, his elk and belongings in the pickup and headed for town. I was to have the meat processed and shipped to his home. He was taking the antlers and cape with him on the plane next day.

I drove up to the Holiday Inn where he had a room and started to pack his stuff to the room when he stopped me and said, "Let's pile it right under this tree. I'll sleep right out here with it so's I'll not miss the courtesy car to the airport."

I guess he did just that. I don't know. One thing I will bet is that Ma and Pa were just as excited as he when they picked him up at that Nebraska airport.

DUDE MEN

People who become outfitters and dude ranchers all have to be a certain stripe of people to make it go. Just anybody can't do it. You have to be of a pleasant personality, a good horseman, a cook, a half-baked doctor and beyond all a psychologist. This is probably one of the most needed traits.

I have known some of the best and most outstanding of all of these characters who have ever graced our industry.

One I'll never forget was Old Cap who had a resort over on Lindberg Lake. He always wore this big old 10 gallon hat, brown in color underneath the dirt and sweat of many years wear. You never saw Cap without this hat. I am very sure he even slept with it cocked over his right eye. Also, he always wore a pair of runover boots. They were his trademark.

One day he found himself in Chicago and decided to call up an old guest. Well, this guest was a man of great importance. He owned a large business and was also a very dignified gentleman. Old Cap saw his place of business across the street and slipped over there and walked into this gentleman's office.

His secretary really came alive when this guy in a plaid shirt and overalls under this tremendous hat just barged in without being announced. She says, "What on earth do you want?"

Cap says, "Where's Bill?"

She says, "Mr. ------- is in a meeting."

Cap says, "Call him out and tell him Cap wants to talk to him."

Now this gal is horrified. She says, "I can't do that."

Cap says, "You call him like I tell you or I'll do it."

All the time Cap is having a ball. He sees she's scared to call her boss. Finally, she dials the phone and asks to speak to her boss. She said, "A rather uncouth man is here. He says his name is Cap."

The door across the room flies open and out races Bill. Shaking Cap's hand, he says, "You old son of a gun, it's good to see you." The secretary stands back in awe. Bill says to her, "You call my car and you take Cap to my house. Call the wife and tell her Cap will be staying with us for a few days."

She grabbed the phone, made the call and took Cap to Bill's house

Howard and his horse Warbonnett.

clear across Chicago. Finally, they became very good friends and in later years she and her family became guests at the lodge.

When people arrived at the lodge, they were usually in a group and the first thing some unsuspecting soul would need was a bathroom. When they unloaded from the old bus, Cap would talk to them spinning yarns, etc., until someone would ask him where the bathroom was. He'd say, "Right over there"and point. Right out in front of the lodge in the middle of the lawn was a nice Chick Sales outhouse. When the unsuspecting client was settled right comfortable, someone would pull the rope and all four walls would fall to the ground, leaving the user sitting on the throne out in the middle of the yard. Now if I had done this somebody would have killed me, but not Old Cap. He could get by with murder and they all loved him for it.

He also had a sign over by the edge of the timber that read with an arrow pointing up the foot trail of a steep rocky hillside: "Lost Mine." When you reached this high rocky point that overlooked the lodge and the lake, there was a pole bench to sit on and a sign that faced you saying, "Darned If I Could Find It Either."

Then there was Old Smoke.

When I was just a kid, he was an outfitter in the early 1900's. Back then you would book a party for not just 10 days but mebby for as long as two months at a time. Smoke was a French Canadian and he loved to start in here at Ovando, travel through the South Fork, then through Glacier National Park, on north to Waterton Lakes and ending up in Vamp, B.C., sometimes.

He was a storyteller deluxe. He would spellbind us youngens with stories of the Old West. He knew people like "Big Nose George," Calamity Jane, Peg Leg and Butch Cassidy, who he claimed he rode with when he was a boy, and also the Champion brothers of the Johnson County Sheep and Cattlemen War.

He had one bad eye that lended a severe look to him along with a big, crooked nose. I never saw this man without a six-gun in the waistband of his overalls. Now I'm telling you he could use it too—the best shot I've ever seen.

He'd tell these stories of robbing a train and outrunning a posse and of Butch Cassidy's going's on. He'd wrinkle up his nose and glare at you with that bum eye and you sure would not doubt him. Well, everyone, even me, took his tales with a grain of salt, thinking the old boy had read too many Ranch Romance or Diamond Dick novels. Finally Old Smoke passed on. I don't know his age but it had to be in the nineties.

A few years afterward I had this party in the South Fork on a fishing trip, quite a large group of men. One of them, "Old John," was from Rawlins, Wyoming. He had a birthday while on this trip; he was 90 years old that day. The cook built a cake and we had a real birthday dinner right down on the big bend of the South Fork about one mile from the Big Prairie Ranger Station.

John was telling us about his childhood days in Wyoming. We were setting around a big campfire. It seemed John's mother was a widow lady who was both railroad station mistress and also ran the post office, trying to raise her family of John and his little sister. She also had a backyard full of chickens and would sell some eggs.

Well someone says to John, "Tell us. What is the most memorable happening in your life in the early days of Wyoming?"

John says, "Well I was a small boy about six years old playing out in the middle of the street. Now Rawlins was a small place with only a road between two lines of buildings then. Into town came this group of cowboys on a run, riding their horses, shooting in the air and laughing and hollering. I'm right in the middle of their way. As they passed me one of them reached down and picked me up and placed me up in front of him on his horse. We rode up and down the road a while, them shooting in the air. Finally they stopped at the saloon.

This guy with the bum eye says, "Son, where do you live?" I pointed and he rode over and sat me down on the station porch. Then he says, "Whose them chickens?"

I says, "Maw's."

He jerks out his gun and shoots six of Maw's chickens, and then says, "Hold my horse." Then he picks up the chickens, goes in and sees Maw. He gave her a 20 dollar gold piece for each chicken and says, "Me and the boys we'll come back for a chicken supper tonight." Sure enough, they did. Now this was the Butch Cassidy's bunch headed for Mexico. They had just robbed a bank. They called this guy Smoke."

Everyone sat around the fire quiet-like and I says, "John, was this guy's last name Deneau?"

John says, "Yes, why?" I told him of the Smoke we all knew and that Smoke had told me the exact same story. Now I never know when to doubt a man's strange story anymore.

After the Johnson County War there was a poster nailed to the depot naming some of the hard cases to leave Wyoming, and Big Nose George and Smoke are the first and third names on the list, so they tell me.

Another friend of mine and to all who knew him was a real dude man, a great storyteller with a special way of using the English language to suit himself and to the enjoyment of everyone who listened. Spike had a way with people and horses alike that cannot be duplicated. He has left us now, but is a legend in Montana's history.

I was at his ranch one time when he had a young fellow riding out some colts. Now he really raised good horses. His pet saying was, "If you've got a good horse, don't sell him for no price. He'll bring your guest back time and again and make you money."

Well this young lad was having a time with this colt. Or mebby the colt was having a good time with the lad. I really don't know, but after bucking the kid off seven or eight times the kid is having a little trouble getting up when this old boy shuffles up to him laying on the ground and says, "Son, if'n you don't learn to get off better you're goin' a ruin that damn colt." Such advice and sympathy!

Then one time in the middle of winter I gets this letter from Chicago. This organization wants me to come work for them. All I have to do is sit in a chair at their meeting posing as a derelict and alcoholic. It was beautifully done, this letter. You had to read it two or three times to figure if someone was pulling your leg. I racked my brains as to who had sent it to me. Finally, I settled on one of my guests from Chicago.

Along about November the next fall, my wife and I were at a Dude Ranchers Convention and were sitting right across the table from our friend Spike and his wife at the president's banquet. The M.C. was speaking when in came a guy and said he had a letter addressed to this guy and had been asked to read it. My friend was the outgoing president of the Dude Ranchers Association at this time. The M.C. got about halfway through the letter when my friend jumped up and pointed at me and yelled, "That's a fake. Here's the Son of a ------ that sent the letter." Well, I did not send them that letter, but I knew right then who had sent it to me.

There was another guy who nicknamed himself Hobnail Tom and it stuck.

Now Tom was a guy who could sell an Eskimo a deepfreeze. A retired professor, he had degrees up both arms. He was a botanist and speaker supreme. When Old Tom gave a speech at some meeting you could hear a pin drop on a pillow. Such a delivery I've seldom seen.

He could really entertain his guests. He knew every plant, weed or flower in the mountains. He'd ride along the trail, one leg wrapped around the saddlehorn, pointing out all day long flowers, birds and what berries were good to eat.

Now Ted and I were camped along the Dry Fork of the North Fork with a fishing party and we knew Tom was coming by that day with a large party. Old Ted says, "We ought to job Old Tom some way today."

I said, "Good idea but what can we do?" We were cutting up some firewood right along the trail when all of a sudden the idea hit me. I says to Ted, "See that big lodgepole tree right at the bend of the trail. Let's cut a hole right through it and see what happens when Tom comes along." Well, I took the power saw and cut a hole about eight inches square right through the tree at an angle you couldn't miss when riding up the trail.

Ted says, "We'd better make it look old." So he smeared the inside of the fresh cut with mud and we cleaned up all of the sawdust. It looked 100 years old.

When we heard Tom's outfit coming along we slipped over and laid behind a log to see what happened. Tom's in the lead riding Old Redwing, his horse, talking to his guests about the worth of wilderness, etc. He rode right past this tree. One of his guests from behind hollers, "Tom, what's this hole in this big tree for?"

Tom wheels Old Redwing around and rides back, looks at the tree and without a pause says, "Oh that's an Indian compass."

"An Indian compass! What do you mean?"

Tom says, "Now you know some people get lost easy in the mountains. Then you'll find a guy every once in a while that always knows where the North Star is. Well, the Indians were the same way. So the chief would send these warriors who had this ability all through the mountains. They cut holes in trees always pointing north and south. Then the other Indians always knew where they were going." Never batted an eye and rode on up the trail.

I always say he could come up with an answer to any question asked him, fast, sincere, even if he didn't know. Right or wrong made no difference, but he always had an answer on his tongue. A born entertainer. A dude man supreme.

Going up Larch Hill with Silver-tip Peak in the background.

OLD CHEESE,

PERSONALITY PLUS

Every human, horse, dog, cat and mule has some sort of personality, some good, some bad and some indifferent. What I'm about to tell you of is an old Airedale dog that really had a personality plus, a Will Rogers of the canine species.

My brother and I were outfitters and ranchers before World War II and were doing right fine. Then along came Hitler and Tojo, who really throwed a monkey wrench in the machinery.

When the smoke all cleared away we found ourselves home, saddled with a four-year indebtedness and having to start out again. We had just spent four years working for Uncle Sam's forces at $21 per month and found. However, we never found anything but experience and you can't get very fat on that alone.

Montana, at that time, was paying $25 bounty on mountain lion, so I figured if I could find some hound pups and hunt cats in the winter-time I could help fill the cupboard and have an income other than just seasonal outfitting. Any other job was like finding hen's teeth. Nobody had any money to spend on labor.

One day we called Dr. Metcalf, a vet from Missoula, to doctor a horse. Naturally, hunting came up in our conversation and I says, "George, do you know where I can get some hound pups?" He said he'd keep his eyes open and left.

Well, one day I gets a phone call and George says, "Say, can you use a three month old Airedale? He'd ought to chase cats."

I said, "I'll come and get him."

This is in late December and real cold. My wife and I had an old Oldsmobile coupe, no heater, but away we go. We picked up this pup and with me and him it was friends upon sight. He was like a turpentined cat when I put him in that car. He took one look at my wife and felt the same way about her as I did. He just had to kiss her about a hundred times in the first six seconds he was in the car. She didn't share his sentiment.

Have you ever been locked in a car with a dog that has been in a kennel for two weeks? Well, if you haven't you can't realize what your nose was really invented for. What a smell! You didn't dare open the windows or you'd freeze, so it was keep them shut and gag your way home over 80

Old Cheese and friend Pelzer

miles of rough, icy country road. Needless to say, by the time we got to the ranch he had softened Marg's heart and was one of the family.

When we let him out of the car, he took my brothers and the rest of the ranch the same way with rush and wiggle and a burst of energy unbelievable. Wendell, a younger brother, says, "Where'd you get that Cheese Hound?" And Cheese it was. He was known throughout Montana, written about in newspapers and national sports magazines. Just last night I saw his picture in a Hunting Annual magazine.

Next was how to train him to hunt. This posed some problem because the trainer is supposed to know more than the pupil. Here's where we lacked, but Cheese took over. As I said, he is a three-month-old pup, just a little feller. We hadn't decided how to start him yet when along came a guy on snowshoes and stopped for coffee.

He says, "Say I hear you got a cat dog. I just saw where a she cat and two youngun' crossed the trail up to the lake.

I looked at Wendell and he says, "Let's go."

We got our snowshoes and Cheese and up the mountain we went. The pup was following our track and when we came to the cat tracks we stuck his nose down in them and said, "Sicum." He sniffed the tracks, walked up, sniffed another and started the awfullest yapping and away he went. We went right after him as fast as we could go. In a half hour we met Cheese coming back to us. We said "Sicum" again. Away goes Cheese.

Soon we came to where he had had the cats up a tree. Well, this went on all afternoon. He'd tree the cats, then come back to see what we were doing. Finally, just about dark, we got to the tree before he left to look for us. It was a big day when we got home for a late supper, three mountain lions, $75, a three-month-old pup and two experienced dog trainers. This was quite a start for such a pup.

We'd hunt lion for bounty in the winter-time, pack hunters in the fall, take fishing trips in the summertime, and Cheese was always there. Everybody loved him. He was the greatest bum of all when it came to lunch on the trail. He'd beg and get part of everyone's sandwich, candy bar, orange. If you could eat it, so would he.

How many mountain lion and bobcats he treed for us I do not know. I have often wished we had kept a record.

While in hunting camp in the fall, things would get a bit dull for him so he'd take off and go visit other hunting camps miles away, then come home. Everyone knew him and loved him. One night it was bitter cold and Old Cheese dropped in for a visit at a neighbor's camp.

One of the hunters called him into the tent and fed him and let him sleep on the foot of his sleeping bag. The next morning, Cheese went hunting with this man, who shot a fine bull elk. When he got back to camp that night he noticed no dog. When the outfitter went to pack out the elk, lo and behold, right on the middle of the elk is Cheese. When they started to pack the elk Cheese says, "No deal." This is a Copenhaver elk, now you guys go get your own. Every time they'd try to come close to the elk Cheese would take 'em, and he meant business. One of his personality traits was being a terrific watchdog. He wouldn't let a stranger come near the house or camp 'til you told him it was all right.

Tom, the outfitter, was trying to think of some way to get the elk away from the dog. They had tried rocks, sticks, etc., but Cheese would chase them off instead. Tom says, "We might as well eat our lunch and maybe he'll leave after a while. I don't want to hurt him."

Then, all of a sudden, he gets a bright idea as he recalls Cheese's taste for lunches. He got the lunch out and called, "Here Cheese, want some lunch," and rattled the paper sack. It was too much for old Cheese. He came over, accepted his share of their lunch, looked the situation over, got up and headed over the mountain for Copenhaver's camp.

I could go on for hours on just such tales of this dog, but by now he's getting old, 14, mebby 15 years, been tore up, sewed up from cuts of mountain lion and horses, broken bones by a grizzly and very rheumatic. He has trouble walking in the summertime.

Three times the last summer of his life, I met him on the trail to hunting camp. Each time I took him up on my horse and carried him home and put him in the kennel.

Late this same year I met Wendell. I was coming out from a hunting trip and Wendell was going in to help break and pack our camp out for the

When we hunted for bounty.

year. Cheese was hobbling along behind Wendell. He said, "Take Cheese home. I didn't know he was behind me." I said, "Wendell, the trail is good and solid-packed snow. Let the old boy go in. He's tried all summer to go into hunting camp. It'll probably be his last trip."

Cheese made it back to camp but Wendell couldn't get him to make one step toward home. He would start off down the trail, hoping Cheese would follow. After three tries he tied up his mule, went back and caught Cheese and carried him on his horse. But as soon as he got down the trail a ways and set him down, he'd take off for camp again. Finally, Wendell went back to camp, left a quarter of elk, made a bed and rode off and left Cheese to his own.

We never seen or heard of him or found any remains the next spring, but while I'm writing this I'm not 20 feet from the spot where Cheese had chosen to spend his last day.

People still talk of "Ole Cheese" and old guests from back east still ask, "Whatever happened to Ole Cheese?"

MILWAUKEE GOAT

A number of years ago we were contacted by the State of Montana Fish and Game Department, asking if we would consider taking the Milwaukee Museum group on a goat hunt. The idea was to collect a family group of mountain goat to be given to the State of Wisconsin for their Museum of Natural History in Milwaukee.

Arrangements were made and the three men arrived. We had as guests a taxidermist, Walt Pelzer, artist and photographer, Bill Swartz, and a sports writer, Mel Ellis, a fine group of young men if there ever was one. We were to hunt the Scapegoat and Danaher country. This is wonderful country—a mountain goat's dream of home. Scapegoat Mountain is big, high and beautiful, stretching out for several miles with long, cliffy ridges running down from the high, cliffy top to the valley floor below, with limestone and malachite lava of red, brown and white, scattered timber, lots of salt grass and lichen and many acres of brushy plants animals love to feed on. It is a huge, rugged country inhabited by elk, mule deer, mountain goat, wolverine, grizzly bear, mountain lion and many smaller creatures of the hills.

It was in the middle of October and beautiful weather. Our object was to get the best of trophies, not just goats. We had to have perfect specimens of each, a nanny, a billy and a kid.

After several days of watching, stalking and glassing, we found just what we wanted in a big, barren nanny. She had an extremely fine, white, long coat with at least 10 1/2 inch black spikes with tips like needles.

Finding a billy proved rough. We found many billies all shaggy and dirty, but nothing with spikes we desired. Finally, Gene spotted a big old billy all alone near the top of Scapegoat on the Cabin Creek Divide. After a hard climb using rope and getting our hunter and cameraman in place, we found upon glassing him that we had the Old Boy we had wished for. He had at least 10 1/2 inch spikes, big and heavy at the base, and his pants hung within six inches of the ground. He was a real trophy if there ever was one. Gene slipped the rifleman up a ravine and to the edge of the slide where the goat was feeding, the sports writer, cameraman and me watching and hoping for a clean kill. Bang! Down went the billy slick and clean. This was the largest billy I've ever seen in the whole goat country that I've hunted in both Idaho and Montana.

A real billy.

When a trophy was taken we would clean all the bones, make measurements and take pictures so the taxidermist could duplicate their bodies as near as possible. Bill, the artist, would not only photograph the area but paint a picture of it. I would set behind him as he painted and point out logs or rocks or mebby a bush he'd miss. He also collected actual specimens of the moss and lichens and bushes. This all took time.

Now we had the nanny and billy. Next came the kid. We had to find a nanny with twins. We did not want to take a lone kid. We'd find some nannies and kids but always the kids were sort of scrubby and not good coated. Now we were playing with weather. We could get rain, snow and fogged-in mountains any day. Also, we'd about used up our time of 14 days we'd planned on.

Late one afternoon I spotted these two nannies headed for a water hole high in the red cliffs of Cabin Creek. After them we went. It was treacherous terrain, steep and with small shale underfoot, kind of like walking on marbles on a hillside. After a couple of hours of crawling, climbing, sliding down ravines and climbing out, we topped the ledge over the water hole and no goat. This water hole was like a well in the cliff. I threw a rock over into the hole and out came two nannies and three kids. The

Goat country. Scapegoat Mountain.

Howard and the Milwaukee billy. Photo by Mel Ellis.

twins were beautiful, snow-white and large for their age. They had a big nanny in prime shape for a mother. This was perfect. I said to the rifleman, "Shoot the one on the right, he's a billy."

He lined up on him then drops his rifle and says, "Howard, I can't do it. You'll have to shoot him." He just couldn't shoot that kid so I shot him with my .22 Ruger Bear Cat."

We stopped to rest with the sun just topping the mountains in the west when Mel said, "This has been a perfect hunt. Only one thing can make it better."

Someone says, "What's that, Mel?"

Mel says, "If a golden eagle would show up." No sooner said than done. We heard an eagle cry, looked up and a pair of beautiful birds circled and circled right over our heads.

Now I must go back and tell you about Mel. Mel was a tough little Italian, just as rough and tough as they come. He had a vocabulary that would stop a teamster. He was always just so tough that nothing in the world could bother him.

After we had rested a little while, we started down off the mountain. I picked up the kid and threw it over my shoulder and as we walked along the nanny and the other kid followed us, blatting. It wasn't pleasant for any of us. This tough writer, Mel, took off down the mountain as hard as he could run, beat us to the horses, got on his horse and took down the trail to camp. About three miles down the trail we caught up to him. He's riding along with the tears running down his face. Now you see it doesn't make any difference how tough a guy is, there is something that will just get to him. Taking that kid was too much for poor old Mel.

Well we made it to camp, a successful hunt almost completed. We arose the next morning to find the mountains fogged in and rain and snow covering the ground.

If ever you happen to be in Milwaukee, be sure and take time to visit the museum and you will see Montana's gift to Milwaukee, three mountain goat feeding on the Cabin Creek Reef of Scapegoat Mountain. It is a beautiful display. You'll love it.

How did you get here? A billy in his summer coat.

On top of Scapegoat Mountain.

CHARACTERS I HAVE KNOWN (DON)

One time Marg and I were visiting some friends. Bill was a graduate of forestry and had in later years become a ranger in the Forest Service. Bill was a real savvy guy with good common sense and became so disgusted with Forest Service management and policies he left the service. He had worked for me for many years as a top hand and guide. Consequently, his wife, Bobbi, had been around the ranch a lot over the years and knew many of the men who had worked for me. We were talking this evening about some of the old times and Bobbi says, "You know, I have never seen a place where so many strange characters gathered over the years."

I stopped and thought. She sure was right and I wondered how come so many had worked for me. All of them down to the last man were the best guides, packers or cooks you could find. I think the reason was they were all independent by nature. All I ever did was tell them what needed to be done and they knew how to do it and did it. I knew their faults and overlooked them, giving them plenty of air.

Don, the mule man, was one character for sure. My brothers and I were in real need of a good guide and a packer who really could handle some rank young mules we had. In the first part of September of '47, a car drove up in the yard by the saddle shed. Out steps this Scotchman about 5 foot 10 inches and 180 pounds. You could see by his hat and clothes and the way he wore them that he'd been around. Well, he'd been around all right. The bar mostly. He was some liquored up.

In his Scotch brogue he says, "Hear you guys need a good man. I'm here. Do I get the job and how much?"

I says, "Can you handle rough stock? We got some new mules that are good but plumb rank."

He comes back, "If'n I couldn't I wouldn't be here."

We sure looked this lad over good, but we needed a man bad and if he stayed on the booze we could always fire him. He never did drink on the job. We settled on a wage, got him settled in the bunkhouse and he says, "When we leavin'?"

I says, "Early in the morning."

Don says, "Where's them hard tails? " meaning the mules.

I says, "Right there in the corral. I'm just finishing shoeing. Don says, "I'll look-see."

This writing brings up so many things about Don that I've forgotten all about for a long time. It's fun. Hope you can enjoy this anecdote.

What a guide and mule man supreme! There was only one made like him; then they threw away the dies. No more. He always said when people would remark about his ability to handle rank stock, "I just says, 'Don, if'n you was a mule, what would you do?' and she usually does."

Now Don would never change clothes. He'd brush his teeth, comb his hair, was always clean shaven and took a bath regular, but he would not let my wife wash his clothes. One time between trips Marg says to me, "You steal Don's clothes tonight and I'll wash them and he'll have clean overalls for the next trip." We did this.

Well, the next morning Don came in for breakfast. Was he mad! "Who washed my overalls?," he says.

Marg says, "I did."

His exact words were, "Do it never again." He tells her how foolish she was and very emphatically informed her, "All washing clothes does is wear them out and they don't ever fit again."

He'd come for a meal, wash his face and hands, comb his hair, and brush his teeth like nobody's business. Then he'd reach in his hip pocket and come out with a snoose can, load his lower lip until it looked like he had a ulcerated tooth. Then he'd sit down and eat his dinner, snoose and all.

One morning Don came into the cook tent and Chauncey, the cook, was cooking breakfast. Now Don had to have his oatmeal mush every morning. He'd fill a big bowl with oatmeal, lay two eggs on top, three or four slices of bacon, a couple of pancakes, and then pour canned milk over all. He'd stir it all up and down the hatch it would go. Well, this morning Chauncey says, "Don, I'm sorry but the mice got into the oatmeal, leaving their droppings in it."

Don looks in the oatmeal box and says, "I always cook it first, then the mouse manure swells up and you can see 'em better to pick 'em out."

Most outdoor men do not read very much but Don read a lot. He carried these books in his duffle and saddle bags. Guess what kind of books they were? All Shakespeare, Tennyson, William Wadsworth and others I didn't recognize. If he found a comic book, dime western or girlie book in camp, right now it was in the stove and in his Scottish brogue, "Why fill your head with that damn rot?"

Oh, yes, he'd cut his own hair. He had a hand clipper and he'd shear his neck and around his ears clear to the skin. Now this would leave a ridge of hair all around his head. He surely looked funny as it was all uneven. Marg was a good barber but Don says, "Nope, I'll do it myself. Then I gets it just right."

This Don was unbelievable. He was stationed at Powell Ranger Station several years. Wrangling his mules every morning was not to Don's liking. Too much work. He figured out if he had a set of bagpipes and learned to play them he would train his mules to come for oats every morning.

Well Old Don bought the pipes and finally found a woman in Spokane, Washington, to teach him this art. It took Don three winters driving back and forth 300 miles to learn to play a tune or two on the pipes. He'd play the pipes and then give the mule some oats. Now a mule is smart and it didn't take long until, when Don started in on his pipes, the mules would start to bray and come running for their oats every morning.

Don was freshly divorced when he first came to work for us. One day while riding along the trail, I says, "What happened to your old lady?"

He says, "She wanted a divorce so I give her the car and house and took down the road."

Don packed mules for the Forest Service in the summer, guided during hunting season and trapped all winter, strictly an outdoor man. I says, "Don, did you just separate or get a real divorce?"

"Nope, we went to the judge and all proper," he says. All is quiet for a while and then he starts laughing sort of quiet-like.

I says, "What's so funny?"

He says, "Well when we gets to this here judge, the judge asks my lady, 'On what grounds are you suing this man?'"

"Grounds," says Don's wife, "I don't want no ground. I just want a divorce, your honor."

The judge says, "No, no, by grounds I mean reason like mental cruelty, nonsupport or adultery."

Don's lady love replies, "Well, judge, I'll tell you the truth. In the summer he smells like mules and in the winter he smells like a damn beaver. I've had it."

"'Divorce granted' says the judge and leaves the courtroom with his fist in his mouth. That's about all there was to it. No alimony, no nothing," says Don.

I could go on a long time about Don but I'll finish up with this classic.

I've already told you about Don's reading. Well, on this trip some non-suspecting guest had packed in a *Playboy* magazine and in it was the story about an angel of the night who ran a house of ill repute in Calumet City up north of Chicago. The story was about what a big name surgeon in Chicago had done to this poor girl with increasing her bust-line with plastic surgery.

One night along about 2 o'clock in the morning I woke up to a gruff, "Howard." I says, "What you want, Don?"

He says, "Know what I'm going to do this winter right after hunting season?"

I sleepily says, "What's that, Don?"

He says, "I'm going to go to Calumet City and visit this plastic-titted whore."

I says, "Go to sleep. You'll forget about it by morning."

Well, hunting season was over and winter was underway, must have been in January. Marg shakes me in the middle of the night and says, "Somebody wants to talk to you on the phone."

"Who is it?" says I.

"I don't know but I think it's Don and he sounds like he's drunk," says Marg.

I get up and go to the phone. "Hello, who's this?" I says.

"It's me, Don," came the answer.

I says, "What you want and where you at?"

Don says, "I'm in Calumet City and I found this plastic-titted so and so."

"You got to be kidding me," I says.

"No I ain't," says Don. "She cleaned me out. Can you send me 50 bucks to get home on?"

"Sure," I says. So he gave me the address of the flophouse. We sent him the money and Don came home.

I said this was the end but I can't leave Don without telling you about his bout with the IRS.

L. B. Johnson was president at this time and his wife "Lady Bird" was on a Clean Up America fling. Congress had set up a huge sum of money to push this plan ahead. Well, that was tax money. This really touched off a button in Don's noggin. He says, "Let them clean up their own mess. I cleans up mine. I ain't going to pay no more income taxes." So he didn't. Well, it went on for several years and all of a sudden the IRS nailed poor Don. He gets a sharp attorney and finds out if he pays part of it in hard cash they couldn't do much. So every year Don would go in and pay them some on his bill in silver, and each time get a receipt and leave.

This went on for a number of years. I'd say, "Don, why don't you pay it off and forget it?"

He'd say, "Tain't the money. It's the principle I cares about."

As I said, this went on for years and Don finally owed $1.33. Marg and I were in Missoula on the 15th of March this year and as we walked by the Federal Building out comes Don from the IRS office. We say, "What you doing Don?"

He says, "Paying my tax."

I says, "Did you get it paid up?"

He says, "Nope. I owes them 33 cents yet."

We visited a bit and parted. Next day in the paper is an article about Don. Seems he got his nose wet in town that night and went home to his trailerhouse to sleep. He must have turned up the gas heater and it did not light because they found Don next morning asphyxiated by the gas.

He's probably laughing up there because he beat the IRS out of 33 cents.

BUD'S BULL

This was back in '53 about the last hunt in November. We had probably about six inches of snow on the ground. We were camped on the Dry Fork of the North Fork of the Blackfoot River at the mouth of Cabin Creek.

Our hunters were a group of fellows from San Fransisco. None of them had ever hunted elk before, but they had hunted mule deer in Utah and the Kaibab in Arizona. Two of them, Bud, a young fellow and John, a gentleman in his 60's, were always bantering each other. Great poker players and forever trying to clean the other guy's pockets or job you some way and get you into a mess of trouble just for fun. You'll hear more about this Bud guy in this book.

On the trip into camp, this betting started over who would get the first and the biggest. Now years ago I learned that record heads are usually killed by chance not hunted for. By the first morning of the hunt the pot had grown to $50 on the first elk killed and $100 on the biggest. I was guiding Old John and Bud had drawn my brother, Wendell. Now Wendell is the best elk hunter I have ever had the pleasure of being around. When no one else can find a bull, Wendell can and it's not just luck.

I remember one hunt so well. We had this guest who was so noisy and clumsy he couldn't walk up a interstate highway without falling down. He'd kick every log he came to and spent more time getting up than he did hunting.

Wendell's hunter had filled his tag and Wendell says, "I'll take Joe to-day and see if I can do anything for him."

Now it was crusty snow and noisy. They picked up this lone bull track right off and took after him. Wendell says to his man, "Now you see my footprints. Well, you put your feet right in them. Don't you look for anything other than where you set your feet. If you break a stick or fall down, this bull will be gone and I'll go back to camp."

He got this old boy to crawl on his hands and knees, but they slipped up on that old smart bull and Joe shot him.

Well, on with my story. You can see I was up against it trying to outdo Wendell and his hunter. Bud was young and John was old.

John and I took off up onto a piece of country we call the bench.

Steve Copenhaver and Sam Wiess with Sam's bull.

Wendell and Bud were north of us about a mile going up the south side of Whiskey Ridge, just across the creek from us.

Well, me and John pussyfooted along for about a half an hour. No tracks that looked fresh. It had started to snow real big, soft flakes. They came down like a big, soft blanket, layer after layer. I walked up to the edge of a nice little park in the heavy timber. My hunter and I stood at the edge, looking for anything that might be feeding here. Nothing. Not a track. We started across the opening. When we were about a third of the way across, I stopped as if shot. Standing right in front of us at 25 yards stood a big six-point bull looking the other way, just like a ghost out of a dream.

"Get him, John," I says, and he levels and down goes the bull. We walked up to this trophy and he was a dandy in the 47-inch class. We had just started to admire him. Neither had said a word. Ker-Powie! Right across the creek where Wendell and Bud had gone we heard a shot, then a pause of a couple of minutes and a second shot. I said, "John we've got the first bull anyway."

John says, "And the biggest."

I says, "Don't be too sure about that. This is a nice trophy but there are bigger bulls in these hills."

"Oh, no," says John, "Bud couldn't shoot one this big."

—80—

I let him have it his way and dressed the bull and caped out the head. Then we headed for camp.

When we strolled into camp and were toasting the hunt with a coffee royal, John was jubilant; he'd won the money both ways. I says, "John, take it easy. You might lose the big bet yet." Well, in walked Bud and Wendell. I took one look at the smile on Wendell's face and I knew he had us hands down when it came to size.

The pot started growing with John really pouring it on poor Bud. John'd bet $10 or $20 and Bud would cover. I saw him looking at Wendell every little bit and am sure I caught a sly wink or two. Now supper is ready and when Bud headed for the kitchen I tell John, "Don't bet no more. You'll lose. Them two are setting you up."

John says, "Why that Hunky ain't smart enough to set old Joe up."

Well by bedtime there was $250 bet on the largest head. Bud paid John his $50 for first place on the time deal.

The next morning Wendell and Bud head out with three pack mules, John and me with two. John says, "What they doing with all three mules?"

I says, "I don't know." But I could guess.

Well, about noon John and I come into camp. I was unloading the mules when I hear John say to the cook, "They got two elk. There's two heads on that one mule."

I looked across the park and here came Wendell and Bud. The lead mule was loaded with the cape on one side and hide on the other and on top was a bull head you couldn't believe. What a spread! And not a point under 18 inches up to 26 inches on the royals. It was such a perfect six-point that when Boone and Crockett measured it there was one point difference in the sides. And it was almost black with six to eight inches of ivory. Such a head!

Bud says, "Where's that elk head of yours?"

John says, "Right there on the ground."

Bud says, "Oh, I'm sorry. I thought that you'd shot a mule buck this morning."

Now John and Bud had hunted for a number of years as partners for mulies and birds all over the Southwest. Well, this ended it. Bud came back for years. John was mad at me and everything Montana had to offer.

What really happened that first morning was that Wendell and Bud had just tied their horses and started to climb up the ridge not 100 yards from their horses when this nice six-point walked right out in front of them from out of a ravine in the hillside. Bud leveled on him and missed him clean. Now Wendell is giving him the bum's rush for being such a poor shot saying, "You miss a bull like that right here on the main trail, then you'll probably shoot some old baloney bull in a thicket of downfall right on top of a high mountain some place and I'll have to spend a day or two packing him out."

Just like that, another bull steps out of the same thicket right in front of them and Old Bud doesn't miss this time. He says to the day he died that he knew there was another bigger bull right there and shot at the first one just to scare him away and make room for the big one.

Bud's bull measured up and was second largest in North America in Boone and Crockett in '53. I truly think it was the most beautiful head I've ever seen.

Top trophies of elk, mountain lion, mulies and grizzly we've taken over the years have always showed up by chance.

You either do or you don't.

A mule on the ground. A real wreck.

HOLLAND LAKE WRECK

Back in about 1957 I was real short on pack stock. I needed 10 more pack horses than I had. I had a big party of 28 people for a trip over Holland Pass, down by Big Salmon and on through the South Fork on a fishing trip. I had packed these men on fishing and sightseeing trips for several years.

Now always I had a fellow named Ted working for me. He was a horse trader deluxe. There are more stories about his escapades than Carter has liver pills. I says, "Ted do you know where I can rent 10 good gentle pack mules or horses?"

He says, "You bet. I've got 12 of them over by Polson. If you want I'll go get them."

I says, "How much?" We agreed on a price. I says, "Now Ted, I don't want a bunch of half broke broomtails."

Ted says, "Oh these are good. Just a little snorty."

I says, "OK, but you and me are going to pack them. Now you make sure they are good."

"OK," says Ted and he takes off after his truck and the stock. Me and the rest of the boys start hauling my mules and saddle horses and equipment over to Holland Lake early the next morning. It's about a 75 mile haul one way and we had to make several trips, so about 7 o'clock I still had a load or two to haul that night. I says to Steve, my son, who was about 12 years old, "You stay here at the corrals and when Ted gets here have him put his stock in that little pen. Now you watch and see if any of them are snaky when he unloads. We'll go get the last loads. You can eat at the lodge."

Now my son, Steve, is quite a boy. He has been going in the mountains with me since he was five or six years old, some years spending almost the whole summer on the trails and in camps with me. He is an excellent rider and horseman and knows all the main trails from one end of the wilderness to the other. Now at 12 he knows more about what's good or bad around a pack outfit than most men I could hire.

Well, when we returned I saw some new stock in the pen but paid no attention and went to unloading my truck and here comes Steve. He says, "Howard, I don't know about those horses of Ted's."

I say, "Why?"

He says, "Well, Ted didn't come. Guy brought them." Now Guy was Ted's dad.

I asked him what Ted was doing because Ted liked old John Barley Corn and I was worried because I had to have him next morning by 4 a.m.

Steve says, "He's looking for four horses he couldn't find."

I says, "Steve, how did they act when Guy unloaded them?"

Steve said, "He didn't use the unloading ramp. He just backed the truck up to the corral and jumped them out."

I said, "Didn't he have halters on them?"

"No," says Steve, "Guy said they're not halter broke."

Right then I knew I had had it. We were in for trouble. Smokie and me went and took a look-see. All of those horses were three and four year olds, and just as owly as you've ever seen. When we walked into the corral, I knew Ole Satan was in on this too. Smokie says, "I'm glad I'm the cook and have a gentle string of mules for my kitchen."

Well, sometime in the night in comes Ted's old truck. He shuts it off and rolls out his sleeping bag. At daylight we're up catching horses and mules and saddling them. I says, "Ted, just leave yours alone. After we get the rest of them on the trail, we'll pack extra case goods and beer on your string."

Everyone was on the trail by about 10 o'clock. I says to Bob, "When you hit Shirttail Park on the head of the Gordon, you make camp cause me and Ted might be late."

Bob says, "Late hell. You'll be there in the middle of the night."

Well old Barney, who owned Holland Lake Lodge back then, says, "Let's go get some coffee before you birds start on that mess of colts." OK, and away we go.

In that catch pen was an old blue mare and six three year old colts. In the truck were a couple of four year olds and a grula mule, a funny blue-gray color. I four-footed the first one and Ted fell on his head and I tied all four feet and we left him laying there. This is the way we went through all the rest of them. Finally, we got them all haltered and tied to trees. Then we'd tie up a hind foot and pack them. In about two and a half hours we had them all loaded.

When we had them all tied together, Ted jumped on his saddle horse and took the lead rope on the mule because he was halter broke. I cut their feet loose, jumped on my saddle horse, grabbed my ketch rope and hollered, "Don't stop 'til they're pooped," and away Ted went on a high lope up the trail. Me, I was right behind slapping that old sour blue mare with my ketch rope. We made it for about a mile before we hit the steep trail and the 200-pound packs started to take their toll. Ted slowed to a nice easy walk and we thought we had it made.

There was a creek coming down the mountain, one waterfall after another in a deep gorge clear down to Holland Lake. We had to cross it right where there was a hairpin turn in the trail. The lead mule hesitated a bit and then stepped right into the water. The rest followed. Now this trail is narrow and steep. That old sour blue mare just set the brakes when she came to the edge of the creek and hauled back, jerking the whole string off the trail and down into the gorge that creek runs in. What a mess! All nine of them colts and packs upside down in the gorge in ice water about two feet deep. Ted still had the cotton pickin' lead mule.

We tied our saddle horses to trees and dove in after those colts. Their bodies and packs dammed up the water 'til it was waist deep. We had to keep their heads up out of the water so they wouldn't drown. We'd cut their halter rope and tie their heads up in the air to a sapling willow or little tree growing out of the creek bank. Ted and I would cut sling ropes as we could see them in the water, dropping the packs. They were all tangled like a bunch of angleworms in a corn can. We would roll one colt off the top of the others, cut his lead rope and roll him down the creek. Sometimes one would get on his feet and walk down the creek. More often, they'd fall on the slippery rocks and we'd roll them again. The water would dam up above us and give us help washing the horses down the gorge. Otherwise, we could not have done it. The sides of this creek were sheer rock from 4 to 10 feet high. We were waist deep in ice water almost all day. One by one, we had to roll them about 150 yards down to a flat just above the lake.

It must have been around 5 o'clock that afternoon when we had the last of the colts on their feet on dry ground. We let them stand and started to pack those wet packs up to the trail. What a job! As I said, we had them loaded with canned stuff and 24 cases of beer. This party loved their beer.

While I'm rolling a pack the last couple of feet to the trail I think we're short one pack animal. I holler at Ted, "Did you see that old sour blue mare?"

"No I didn't," says he.

I holler from the trail, "You come up the creek and I'll go down."

"OK," he says.

Well, I just started down the creek through the tag alder brush and here that old heifer is. She is standing spraddle-legged on the rocky ledge, her front feet on one side of the creek and her hind feet on the other. I call to Ted and he comes. "How the hell are we going to get her down from up there?" he says.

Finally, we get my axe and clear all the brush and trees out from in front of her. Then Ted takes my ketch rope, ties it around her neck, gets his saddle horse and dallies around the horn. I says, "Now when I yell, spur your horse. I'll beat the hell out of her and mebby we can jump her across the creek."

I got me a good shillelagh and yelled· I really hit this old girl across the rump. She never even waited for Ted to pull. She just gave a little hop and was standing on the trail. I could have killed her. Her packs were still

A wreck along the trail.

hanging in good shape; we didn't even have to adjust them.

Now we still had four packs of beer to pack up the hill. We could hardly move. We were in worse shape than the stock. All of a sudden a voice from up on the trail hollers, "You boys need some help?" and down the hill comes this guy. He's about 6 foot 2 and four feet across the shoulders. I couldn't believe it. He passed me, grabbed the last pack up on his shoulders and as he passed me, picked up my pack and ran up the hill to the trail. He says, "Are there any more down there?"

I says, "No," and down the trail he goes. I never saw him before or after, but I'll never forget him. Old Ted and me ended up back at the Lodge, patching up pack saddles and gear. We ate a lunch with Barney, slept a couple of hours, and then headed out. We had no problem saddling those ponies this morning. We went back up the trail, loaded the packs on those colts—one of us on either side. No foot ropes this time. They really gave us no trouble after that and we caught up with the party about 10:30 that morning.

We moved camp on down to Big Prairie, had two days lay-over for fishing. Old Ted and me and those colts sure had earned a rest and we took it.

Now I'm sure old Ted borrowed those colts out of somebody's pasture because all of the brands were strange to me.

I've got to throw in this little episode right here. This happened right on this trip when we left Big Prairie to camp the next day at Little Salmon. After breakfast and the kitchen string was loaded, I took off with the guests down the trail, leaving Ted, Steve and the rest of the crew to load and bring the duffle and rest of the camp. We were packing 32 mules and horses on this trip. Along about three in the afternoon, in comes Steve with his ten mules. Half an hour later Redhair shows up with his string. I says, "Where's Ted?"

He says, "Some guys showed up and them and Ted were having a beer when I left. He told me to go ahead and he'd catch me."

Now we have had supper and still no Ted. I saddle my horse and take up the back trail to look for him. I'm about five miles from camp on Murphy's Flat when I meet Ted. He's riding along whistling a soft tune, not a care in the world. When he saw me he says, "You old _____. Where you camped at? I've been lookin' for your tracks all afternoon."

I says, "Ted, you're drunk. There's 40 some head of stock makin' tracks up this trail. Now if I was to walk across this grassy flat barefooted you wouldn't slow up your horse to follow me."

When we got to camp everyone ran out to meet us saying, "What happened? What happened?" Ole Ted, with his hat cocked over one eye, sets on his horse and remarks, "Four hours late and two cases of beer short." Everyone laughed and jumped in and helped unload the mules.

You could get so mad at this guy you could kill him and then he'd come up with something funny. Now, a man can't laugh and stay mad.

Donna Copenhaver packing out a bull elk.

Tim Green, a top guide and friend, with a bull elk.

POP

He's dead and gone now but I know he must be on a hunt in the Great Happy Hunting Ground where we all hope to go when our time comes.

Old Pop was a high pressure businessman in the aeronautical line. His company developed and manufactured many of the new aeronautical devices that helped us win the Second World War. Consequently, he was busy every hour of the day and night when people could find him.

He took pride in the fact that he was a farm lad from upstate New York. One day he was helping his father bale hay with an old horse-driven stationary baler. It wasn't feeding the hay fast enough so Pop took his foot to push the hay into the plunger. His leg got caught and he suffered a broken ankle. He ended up with one leg two inches shorter than the other. He always walked with a distinct limp. When we were out hunting, he always accused me of going around a sidehill so his short leg was downhill. He was always ready with some light-hearted but profound quip.

We might be busy running the ranch or something else and from out of the east you could hear this high whine of that 450 Jacobs in his old single engine Beechcraft when he cut the motor above the high divide and dropped 5,000 feet—Ker-Boom—sitting down in our pasture. Someone would say, "Here comes Pop."

We'd greet and he'd say in his cockney English brogue, with his nose all wrinkled up, "The pressure got too much. Any elk or fish hereabouts?" And off to the mountains we'd go.

I recall one trip such as this when myself, a friend from California and Pop went hunting. It was in October. Beautiful Indian Summer. The first day out I called up a bull. We were on a high, rocky point jutting out over some heavy virgin spruce, just a narrow strip about 50 yards wide and mebby 200 yards long running along a little stream. This bull had a harem with him and there were two or three other bulls hanging around bugling their heads off and trying to steal his cows. Such a concert of nature! No one could help but become excited and keyed up who has ever witnessed such a deal.

Well finally the old boy walked out on a rocky ridge right below us. Pop levels down with his old .35 Remington pump and lets him have it. Like a flash, Mr. Bull Elk hits the brush again. Now I'd been around a few hunting trips and I knew he'd hit his target. Pop says, "I'm too pooped and nervous. I missed."

I says, "No, you got him."

He says, "No I didn't. I should have taken a day or two to rest and forget business problems."

Says I, "Pop you set right here now and watch. I'll climb up above and come down through the thicket and drive him out if he's not already down." He agrees and off I go, leaving Pop on sentry. Now Pop was one of the most dedicated hunters I have ever known. He loved to just hunt. If he got something, fine, if not, fine, but to shoot and wound an animal and not get it would break his heart.

When I got in the thicket, sure enough, there's the bull, mortally wounded and me with only a .22 handgun. The only thing I could do was yell at Pop and goose the bull his way. Like dynamite, the bull jumped and ran straight to where Pop stood guard right out in the open. I hollered and yelled but no shots, no Pop. I ran after the bull, shooting with my little .22 hoping to get Pop's attention. The bull ran past where Pop sat leaning against a tree. When I got there he jumps up and says, "Where?" I showed him the bull fast disappearing down the ridge. Like a flash that old .35 Remington hit his shoulder. Ker-Boom! He had his bull.

With a wrinkled up nose and a bright twinkle in his eyes, says he, "See, Howard, I told you I needed some sleep and rest. In all, Pop and his friends made 19 hunting trips with us over so many years.

When World War I came along a group of young aviators went up to Canada and joined the Royal Air Force making a real name for themselves as the first fighter squadron in the world. When the U.S.A. entered the fight against Kaiser Wilhelm of Germany, Uncle Sam says you boys come home. We must start our own Air Force and that they did. The stories they told around camp would make a book.

These men had great camaraderie and formed lasting friendships. They all made significant contributions to the aviation industry and became very successful businessmen. They formed an organization called "The Quiet Birdmen" or "QB's," a very selective group with a large number of hours of solo air-time required to join. They held regular meetings and took care of widows and children of fallen members.

During World War II, I was injured and afterwards I was having lots of difficulty with my back and legs. I was getting no help here. They insisted I come to Cleveland, Ohio, and go through the clinic and have a bone specialist study my injuries. After an extensive time at the clinic and they had told me all they'd found, I was to leave for home. I went to the office and asked for my bill, but was told there was nobody by my name registered in the clinic. When I tried to pay, these men whom I knew had picked up my bill; they told me, "In our organization we have a rule: When we see someone who really needs help, we help them. When you can repay this debt, look around and help someone else." This I have tried to do and I feel good about it.

Another time I invited Pop to be my guest on a fishing and sightseeing trip. We were taking a group of girls down the South Fork, up White River, over the China Wall, down the Sun River and back over the Continental Divide to Danaher and back to the ranch. The whole trip was about 120 miles with some excellent fly fishing, which Pop loved, and beautiful, spectacular scenery.

I was breaking in a string of new mule colts. One of them, a pretty black mule, was just plain wild. We would have to tie up a hind foot and hobble her every time we packed or unloaded her. No matter what we tried she just got wilder. When we got over on the West Fork of the Sun River, she just quit us one night. We laid over a day and looked for her but to no avail. Pop kept saying, "You boys are wasting your time. When we get to the Danaher she'll be grazing out on the meadows."

We loaded up and left next morning, Pop way out in the lead. As we came into the lower Danaher Meadows I saw Pop kick his horse in the ribs and head for the willows down by the creek. He disappeared in the willows. Suddenly, here comes Pop and that old saddle horse was flat out moving and right behind him was a big cow moose just as black as the mule.

Pop said he saw her in the brush and thought he'd found our mule. He decided he'd run her up to the corral and really have the laugh on us. When he busts around that bunch of willows the calf was nursing. It didn't take long for Mama Moose to send Pop on his way.

Now Pop always liked his little snort every once in a while. While on this trip he'd always dig out a jug in the evening and have a couple of highballs. We had pulled into Brushy Park on the head of White River this afternoon and I was busy setting up camp. Every little bit I'd get the faint sniff of Scotch whiskey in the air. I walked around a clump of trees and here is Pop hanging his clothes all around his sleeping bag on any tree or brush that came handy. The pack mule carrying his duffle had bumped a tree, breaking a fifth of Scotch in his duffle bag. I says, "Did it cut you short on your cocktails, Pop?"

He answered, "Nope. I always carry some spares. If'n I didn't I'd be chewing a sock." A sip of booze is pretty handy to relieve the strain at the end of a day's ride. Another time another fellow was packing his duffle for just such a trip and decided the safest place for his booze was to shove his two fifths into one of his hip boots. Doing so he folded the top down around the leg of the boot and stuffed it into his duffle bag. Now as the mule walked along the two bottles keep jarring together, breaking both of them. When we got to camp, this old boy had a hip boot full of whiskey. He asked the cook for a kettle and a towel which he spread over the top of the kettle. He then emptied his boot into the towel straining out all the broken glass, salvaging the booze. I says, "Bud, how does she taste?"

Bud says, "A little like a sweaty sock but it still has some kick."

Another fellow who always came on the hunts was Kemp. Now Kemp

The meat pole is full. Dry Fork camp.

was an albino. He wore glasses about a half inch thick and even with them he couldn't recognize you at four feet. He insisted on a private guide each year and would hunt from daylight 'til dark every day. He could not see an elk at 20 feet but he really loved to hunt anyway.

One day there was about eight of us riding down the valley when we spotted a bunch of mule deer feeding on a hillside not far above us. The hunters jumped off to shoot at two good bucks that were in the group. Old Pop hollers, "Don't shoot. That's Kemp's buck." He got Kemp lined up, showing him the right direction to point his rifle. Kemp aims and shoots. You won't believe it but he hit that buck dead center. What a deal! We packed out Kemp's deer and went back to camp. The rest of the day was spent in toasting Kemp's shooting ability and the buck. I have never seen such an elated hunter in my life. He told me he had hunted for over 25 years and this was the first game he had ever gotten himself. He knew it was his because no one else had fired a shot.

Pop had a saying, "If you can show me a cow pasture I haven't landed in, I'll do it tomorrow." He was the oldest licensed pilot living at that time. He said, "All these new fangled gadgets foul me up. If'n I get lost there's always a highway or railroad track to follow. They got to go someplace." These old pilots flew by the seat of their pants. Any landing they could walk away from was considered a good landing.

Part of the country Howard outfits in.

Well, this year I'm speaking of Pop, his wife, Mom, as she was known, and his secretary, Annabelle, took off toward Seattle the day after the packtrip in that old Beechcraft. When they hit the coastal range of mountains the weather was socked in and Pop dropped down and was flying the railroad down to Renton where the Boeing Aircraft plant was. He cut a turn in the canyon too wide and ran into the mountainside. The crash was fatal to all three of them.

Pop had the ability to make every person feel like he was giving them his undivided attention. He noticed everyone down to the least choreboy and always remembered them. He made it a point to have a conversation and find out how each one was getting along. He had genuine appreciation for anything that was done for him.

Our little community of Ovando thought so much of Pop they showed up wishing us to express their condolences to his family and friends back in Cleveland, Ohio. He was a great man who surely left his mark in the aeronautical field and also our small world.

Howie Fly and Pete Lineburger, top hands.

TONY

This was way back when I had booked this party of men from Long Island, New York, to hunt the headwaters of the Bitterroot River. We were camped just under the Idaho line on Overwich Creek. This was prime elk, mule deer, moose and mountain goat country with lots of open grassy areas but steep as a cow's face.

The gentleman who arranged the hunt was Tony. He said, "We are truck farmers from Long 'Giland'." They all spoke in a lingo of broken Italian and English, hard to understand. Now Tony says, "I'm a big man. I weigh 345 pounds."

Boy, that stopped me. In that rough country I'd need a D8 cat to haul him into camp. Anyway I says, "That's OK, you'll make it. I'll meet you at the airport in Missoula, but tell me what you look like so I can recognize you when you get off the plane."

Tony says, "Just you look for a big guy with a big banana nose. I have the original banana nose of all Italians."

Boy, did he have a real one. Just like twin bananas with a bulb on the end. He was over 6 foot and weighed in at 375 pounds and he'd never ridden a horse in his life.

It seems all of these boys had been gardeners, raising vegetables for sale in New York. When the city or state decided to build the new bridge across to Long Island all their truck farms were in the way. So Tony, the kingpin of this settlement, sold all the land to the bridge builders for some real big cash and decided to take his henchmen on a hunting trip. Not one of them knew what to expect. What they lacked in hunting experience was well overshadowed by enthusiasm.

As I said, Tony was big and what I needed was a big horse for him, something in the draft horse size, probably, heavy-boned with plenty of feathers around his feet. I had a red roan horse that a friend of mine really liked. So one day when I saw C.B., I says, "You got a big old work horse you'll trade me for that roan?"

C.B. says, "I sure have. He's a sorrel and dog gentle. I'll go home and get him."

C.B. has several teams, all matched pintos or roans. Now C.B. knows how to put the big gentle on a green horse and I know this horse found this out too. Along after dark that night, in comes C.B. with my horse. He says, "He's gentle but don't rein very well."

I says, "That's OK if he'll just go straight down the trail and pack a big, big man."

This horse was a sorrel with a flaxen mane and tail. I called him Cotton. He'd weigh in at 1,500 pounds and could walk like a machine, also very gentle and friendly. When it came to reining, that was something different. You could pull his head up in your lap and he'd go straight ahead. This was all right for on the trail one horse walks right behind the other anyway. All I needed was stout transportation for Tony. Cotton was one of the best dude horses I have ever owned. He just seemed to like to have people ride him. He sort of took care of them. Little kids or big men made no difference to Cotton. He just headed out and done his job.

We picked up Tony and his party and drove to the jumpoff at the end of the road. Smokie was there with the stock all ready to head for camp. We were on the Saddle Mountain Divide and it was six miles down to camp. It was a real steep trail down Shields Creek. We got everyone loaded and the packs on the mules and down the trail I started. After a bit, I looked back to see how Cotton and Tony were making it. Tony was stiff as a poker, pulling on the bridle reins. Old Cotton was shaking his head trying to keep up and Tony was white with fear.

I stopped and went back to him. I tried to explain and show him how to ride better but he couldn't loosen up. Finally, I pulled the bridle off Cotton and says, "Now Tony, just stick your feet ahead so your weight is on your feet. Sort of lean back and look at the scenery just like as if you were in a taxi cab. Don't pay any attention to Cotton and you'll enjoy the ride." Well, Old Cotton fell in right behind my horse and we had an enjoyable visit and ride on into camp.

When I got Tony down off Cotton, he says, "From now we do what Cotton do," and that we did for 10 days.

One day we all went up on top of Pickett Mountain. There was a big plateau on top that had burned off a few years before and the elk liked to feed up there. Most of the timber was flat on the ground, all small lodgepole, real tough to walk through. Off to the southwest end was a deep and steep canyon that dropped off into Overwich Creek, all heavily timbered. When you jumped elk anywhere on the burn they'd always dive for this canyon and you'd never see them again. You had to beat them to this escape route. When we topped out that morning, there was several bunches of elk feeding across the burn for about a mile or so. I said to Pat, "You sneak Tony over to the south rim and me and Smokie will slip around to the north side. When we shoot or jump them, you'll be right in their way to go down Overwich."

Now Tony doesn't travel very fast on foot, so he and Pat are a little short of their spot when Smokie's guy shoots a nice bull. As I said before, all the elk head south for the rim as fast as they can run. As they pass me, my hunter gets his.

Packing out of the Danaher Valley in the Bob Marshall Wilderness.

Pat sees they are not going to be set by the time the elk hit the rim so he says, "Follow me, Tony. Run, Tony," and Pat takes off on a high lope to head the elk. Tony's doing his best but all of a sudden he hooks his toe on a pole and falls flat on his belly. I'm busy dressing out an elk when I hear someone hollering at me. I look way across the burn and see Pat waving his hat at me. I glass him and I can't see Tony. Something must have happened—mebby a heart attack.

Now a number of years before, a fire had burned all of the timber on this high plateau. It was a crown fire which burns all the boughs off the trees, leaving the tree stand bare and dead. This stand was small lodgepole pine, very thick and about three inches in diameter. Wind had blown most of it down by now, leaving a total mess on the ground. You had to step between the small poles when you walked.

Well, Tony and Pat took off at a run to head the elk. Tony tripped and fell, hitting his nose on a log on the ground. Blood was running all over his face and I was trying to stop the bleeding when Tony says, "It's all right. This old banana has been broken lots of times."

About that time out of a draw comes a five-point bull running right past us. Pat hollers, "Shoot him, Tony."

Tony is sitting on the ground. He picks up his rifle, wipes the blood out of his eyes on his sleeve and shoots his bull, saying, "Now I've got this damn blood all over my gun and scope."

He also had a moose license so after a couple of days rest to let his nose and black eyes heal up a bit, I says, "Tony, let's go and fill that moose tag." So away we went.

I found a big old bull and two cows in a swamp around a lake. The lake was in a narrow canyon filled with big rocks, brush and lots of wild gooseberry vines growing about waist high. This was really tough walking. Your feet and legs were always tangling up in the vines and rocks.

We were just about in position to shoot the bull moose when Tony climbs up on top a big rock and sits down. Thinking he needed a rest, I stopped for a little bit. Tony says, "Howard, did that bull ever do anything to you?"

I says, "No."

And he says, "Me neither. Let's just watch him and not do nothing to him."

So we sat and watched Mr. Bull and his cows all afternoon. Then we went back to camp, Tony as happy as if he'd shot a new world record bull.

A good hand warmer. Campfire on the South Fork of the Flathead River.

STARTING A FIRE

This is one story I know you will take with a bit of salt. I'm sure it will be hard to believe. Now, let me tell you something. If you were in the outfitting business, you would not have any problem swallowing it. Personally, I can name a crew of seven men who would verify this.

Ralston Purina Company used to pick professors and teachers from all over the U.S.A. and give them a 12-day packtrip through the Bob Marshall Wilderness in Montana. We would outfit them on these trips. Ralston Purina Company would pay us and it was used as an advertising promotion deal. We took two trips a year each summer, 25 guests to the trip. The questions we were asked were unbelievable, sometimes.

One trip was in June every year. Now, you can experience some mighty cold and wet weather in the hills at this time of year. We pulled into Big Prairie on the South Fork of the Flathead River one afternoon. It had rained all night and most of the day with a cold spring wind. Everyone was wet and I mean cold. Smokie, the cook, and I were trying to set up the cook tent and stove, etc., and get supper going.

Now all of my dear guests huddled under the fly where we were setting up our camp. To the last one, they were going to be first around that stove. No offer of help, just in the way, bitching and moaning in their discomfort.

My son, Steve, and another small boy in the party were asking, "What can we do?"

I says to them, "See that old log down there on that sandbar?" You guys gather all the old limbs and dead brush you can get and pile it by that log. Then I'll set it on fire and mebby these people will get out of our way."

In no time at all, here comes Steve. "Howard, is that enough wood?"

I looked up and here was a group of our guests all carrying brush and limbs to the fire. Now, they really had a big pile. I dug in the pack and got out a can of light gas, filled a pea can and went down to the pile of wood.

By now that old log looked like a grandstand at a rodeo, lined with people like crows around a dead horse. I asked them to step back as I was going to set a fire and that it would start out with a bang and mebby scorch some of them. Not a soul moved, just sat there and looked at me like I had holes in my head. I asked again. No response.

I just threw that can of gas in the bottom of the pile and lit a match right behind it. Ker-Boom! went the fire and over backwards went the people, running over one another to get out of the way. Well, I went back to the kitchen and to work.

After supper a couple of professors and their wives called me off to the side and asked if I'd show them how I started the fire.

I said, "OK. You pile me up a small pile of brush." I went and got a can with a little gas in it and all of a sudden I realized here's my chance for a joke so I says, "Now keep this under your hat and don't spill my trick. First you must have damp wood. Then you take a can of water in one hand and a match in the other. You throw the water under the wood and make sure you throw the match right behind it so as when the water settles through the wood your match is lit and already there. This causes something like spontaneous combustion in dust and Powie, you've got a fire." I showed them how, using the gas, and walked off and got myself busy, momentarily forgetting the lesson.

When we hit camp the next day my friends piled up some wood and threw water and matches till about half of the party was in on it. Finally, here they came for me to demonstrate this thing again.

Smokie overheard and hollered, "Howard, help me a minute."

I says to the guests, "Pardon me, I'll be right back." Soon I returned with my own can of gas, threw it on the pile of wood and a match right behind it and "boom" goes the fire.

Now the payoff. For six more days on this trip my friends soaked down wood and almost ran us out of matches with me demonstrating the fire-starting every night. No one, not one of the help or guests that knew better ever said a word.

These people went home and I'm sure must still believe in spontaneous combustion with a can of water and a country match.

HELENA WILDERNESS RIDERS

For 25 years we rode the trails from one end of the Scapegoat and Bob Marshall Wilderness Areas from east to west and north to south before it was ever designated as wilderness. We were the "Helena Wilderness Riders" and ride we did. I would send the men with the packstrings by main trails to spots where we planned to camp. Me and the riders would cut cross-country, making our own trails lots of the time. These men all loved the high, rough back country and I tried to show them as much new country each year as possible. They also loved to fish some of the main streams, so we would plan the trips to travel high and camp as much as we could where there was good fishing. This meant some days of up to 25-mile rides. They were truly "wilderness riders."

Our dear friend Dunk Mosier of the Forest Service organized the first group as a show-me trip. Many of the first riders came every year 'til Father Time slowed them down. There were Fritz Gannon, Leif Erickson, Dunk Mosier, Neil Livingston, Buzz Palmquist, Bob and Bill Lamont, Bob Stevens, Carl Berry, Bud Ozmun, Bob Clary, John Stephenson, Newell Gough, Henry Loble, Chick Sales, Gib Semmes, John Vance and many more. If I wrote all their names down I'd have no room for a yarn. These were men from all over the U.S. Don't let me forget our good doctors, Wormy and Louis Dyll from Texas.

This was an 8- to 10-day pack trip that sometimes required 70 to 80 head of horses and mules, with five or six packers, cook, etc,—no small deal until later years. There were always from 20 to 28 guests or riders. We really had a good time and formed some friendships that have outlasted some lives. We all still think of those who have crossed the Big Divide and raise a toast to them each trip. For some of those who have left us and took another trail, we named and put signs on trails such as Arkwright Creek on the upper Monture and Galusha Point in the Scapegoat Wilderness Area. These markers are the favorite spots of these men along the way.

Like I said, these men came from all over the country so we always had some Southern boys along. Every night at camp up would go "Old Glory' on a pole and on the other side of the cook tent up would go the Confederate flag.

With much good-natured ribbing and cocktails and toasting to both flags, things would get going around a blazing bonfire. After supper was over someone would start a song and this would run 'til late at night, everyone signing his favorite tune—some of the roughest quartets you ever heard. There were five who really harmonized and could do a fine job together. Many's the night I've went to sleep enjoying their music after the rest of the singers had gone to sleep. One bad thing was, some evenings they would imbibe a bit too much and would hunt up every member of the group and before you could go back to sleep you would have to sing *Good Night Ladies* with them.

Right here I will print the words of a song I dearly love. It was written by Doc Carl Berry and I only wish you could be out under the stars and hear Doc, Neil, Newell and Clary sing this. I can still hear them and the wind in the trees, accompanied by the rush of the South Fork River.

OH, DANAHER

To be sung to the tune *Oh Tannenbaum*
Dedicated to the Helena Wilderness Riders

I'm ridin' to a land I know
Where game abounds and campfires glow.
It's in Montana's Wilderness
A place that's blessed by GOD's caress.

CHORUS

Oh Danaher—Oh Danaher
Take me back to the Danaher
Where the deer and elk all run free
Where the pine and fir reach out to me.

Oh that's the place that I love best.
Oh Danaher—Montana wilderness.

The mountains bound a wide prairie green
Where native trout play in a stream.
The switchback trails lead to passes high
Where a man can hear the eagle's cry.

CHORUS

We riders come from distant lairs
To ride these trails and leave our cares
We toast this land on every score
May GOD keep it wild—forevermore.

Buzz and Neil shipwrecked on a Helena Wilderness Riders trip.

Breakfast came every morning by 6:30 or 7:00 o'clock and everyone was ready for another day in the saddle. These men were from every walk of life. Some were doctors, lawyers, bankers, judges, senators, ranchers, businessmen to name a few, but never a preacher. This outfit was too rank for them, I guess.

One fellow, Neil by name, always showed up with special clothes for the group. You never knew what to expect. I have seen them heading for the ole swimming hole along the river for an afternoon swim, Neil wearing a black swallowtail coat, silk top hat and black bow tie with towel and washcloth draped over his arm followed by Buzz with a butler's white jacket and red bow tie, with his ever-present camera hanging over his shoulder, and big dark glasses. Otherwise they were naked! On one such occasion, unknown to them, an outfitter's wife was having a cup of coffee as these two clowns marched by the kitchen fly. Needless to say, she visited us no more.

Then one year they decided to pack in a couple of rubber rafts and when we'd hit the big river they would float downstream to where we were going to camp that night, usually four men to a raft. Two would walk and fish downriver for a mile or so and those floating would tie up the raft and fish ahead. Sort of a walk and tie deal. It was a very good way to fish and cover a lot of river without walking all the way. Besides, it was a lot of fun floating the river.

But all good things have to come to an end. They got to leaving the

The whole gang of Helena Wilderness Riders on top of the world at the Continental Divide.

boats somewhere above camp or on down the river and the next morning when we were packing to move camp we couldn't find the boats, so I'd have to send a couple of men after them with a mule. They were heavy and needed two men to load them, making us late to get on the trail with the pack mules. One of the packers got the idea of laying along the river with a pellet gun and shooting holes in the rafts right at the water line. Then the floaters would have to let out the air and patch their boat. It sure didn't take much of this to discourage packing in the boats. Until they read this, they have not known what punched so many holes in those rubber rafts.

Another year we planned this trip into a far north part of the Bob Marshall. We would truck all our stock, equipment and groceries to Swift Reservoir north of Choteau and pack in over the Big River meadows and down the Middle Fork of the South Fork, then over Sun River Pass and out to the road at Klick's at the Gibson Reservoir on the Sun River.

The first night we camped at Big River Cabin, a beautiful high valley surrounded by high cliffy peaks, When we turned our horses and mules out to graze for the night, a nice old she grizzly came walking right up the creek and face-on to our stock. What a stampede of horses and mules! Now the boys rounded them up and got them settled down in a side canyon and came in for supper and bedded down for the night. This one gentleman, Bob Stevens of Stevens' Textiles, owned a big cow outfit over at Two Dot, Montana, and he was forever ribbing me about my cowboys. He'd say, "you should see my cowboys at work," and stuff like that. Now I had the best of men, none better in the business.

Well, the next morning the bottomland was all fogged in. You couldn't see any distance at all. The boys were hunting horses and I could hear the bells on the leaders, but could not see them any place. Finally, a light wind came up and was drifting out the fog. All of a sudden, far to the north, I spotted the horses. They were high in the cliffs all strung out on a goat trail. I got my binoculars and could see two of my boys climbing up the rocks and turning them back down the mountain. I ran over and roused Bob in his sleeping bag and gave him the glasses. I says, "Look up at that peak where the sun is just hitting. See them horses. Would your cowboys climb up there and wrangle?" Old Bob looks up there and shook his head. He took another look and said, "If I had cowboys like that I'd kill the sons of bitches," rolled over and went back to sleep. That old she grizzly had spooked that stock up the mountain clear to the goat trails.

One trip stands out in my mind very vivid. We were camped at Little Salmon, one of the most beautiful places on the whole South Fork.

After supper a few after dinner drinks were served from the bar and the party progressed to a high note, when in came Steve and Howie with a horse that had stumbled, fallen and cut a long gash down his face. At one place it was punctured clear through into the nasal passage and had to be sewed up.

We had a veterinary along on the trip, so I broke into the party to get him to do the job. Right now I had four doctors and one vet all very much under the influence ready to help, each with his own little black bag. The vet was trying to sew up the wound and the other four were doing their thing, five doctors and one poor old horse, each cussing the other because of his lack of knowledge. It almost became a fist-fight but we'll deem it to a comedy of errors. The horse lived through it and his face healed up without a scar of any consequence.

Now one of these riders, Doc Carl Berry by name, had a very well-used hat that had an Indian design made of porcupine quills on the front. Over the years he had lost a number of quills so he was desperate to get some new ones. We were riding down Dwight Creek when I, in the lead, spotted this old porky ambling off through the grass. I rode back to Carl and grabbed his hat off his head, ran to the porky and hit with the hat. Well, Mr. Porky whammed that hat with his tail, filling it with quills. I took it

The old-timers line up at Half Moon Park on the Sun River.

back to Carl and said, "Here are your new quills and a new design." He put it on his head and away to camp we went.

We'd got about a mile or so when Carl started to complain about getting saddle sore. We ribbed him and rode on to camp. When we reached camp, Carl could hardly ride or walk either. Being a doctor he set about doing something about it. Lo and behold, some of those quills had fallen off the hat and he had sat on them, driving them good and deep. It was now Carl's turn to be the patient of a vet and three well-oiled doctors, who each had his own remedy for porcupine quills in the butt. It was quite a sideshow for the rest of the members and crew. With much profanity and good-natured harassment, the job was completed.

We rode out to the ranch the next day and to a big supper and party at the Montana Club in Helena. Carl was late as he had been to a doctor in Helena to see if he could get the remainder of the quills out. Now this very sober doc says, "It will take a few days, but they will soften and quit hurting." The other day I called Doc Berry to get his permission to use his song *Oh Danaher* in this story and his last words were, "Don't you write about my porcupine quills. I still have them in my leg."

FOUR GRIZZLY GULCH

Many years ago, now, we had a pair of hunters, Tom and Joe, who came every year. Both men were really excellent hunters and would walk as far every day as the normal man would in two or three. They always ended up with a bull elk, buck deer and very often black bear. All they ever wanted to eat was fried spuds and onions with a piece of meat. They'd never take a lunch claimed a man couldn't hunt good on a full belly. Sort of like a couple of coyotes.

This year I have in mind, Joe was going after a goat, but Tom says nothing but a grizzly bear if it takes 'til Christmas. We were hunting the Scapegoat Wilderness Area, camped on Cooney Creek.

This Cooney Creek country can only be pictured by seeing it. It lays on the extreme headwaters of the North Fork of the Blackfoot River. Cooney Creek starts out of snow banks and springs, rising right out of the cliffs of Olsen Peak and then dropping down from 9,000 foot elevation above timberline, Scapegoat Mountain on the north and Olsen Peak on the south. The side of the mountains are steep and rough. Some of it was burned off in the early 1900's, leaving grassy hillsides with strip timber in between. There are several sharp canyons running from the top of Olsen to the floor of the little valley. One of these is Four Grizzly Gulch. When you get to the 6,000 foot level you run into a dense growth of jack fir, a dwarf sort of bush so thick you can't walk through it except on game trails. From a distance it looks like moss. It is usually about four to six feet high.

Well, Joe got his goat and a nice bull elk and after 10 days went home. Old Tom had seen nothing but grizzly tracks. He says, "I'm going to stay another 10 days," so we said OK and left him and the cook in camp while we all went out after the next party.

When we got back in three days with the new group, I didn't see Tom anywhere. I asked the cook, "Is Tom still out hunting?" Tom would never hunt with a guide. He was a loner.

The cook says, "He's in his tent. He's been there since yesterday, won't talk and don't come to eat. Just sits in there."

"Is he sick?" says I.

"No, he says he's fine," the cook says.

Now after giving Tom plenty of chance to come out and tell he if he's mad, sick or what, I finally goes into his tent and says, "What's wrong with you Tom?"

Tom says, "I just lost my manhood."

"Lost your manhood? What you talking about?"

"Well, it's this way. The day you left I went back up Cooney Creek to where I'd seen those grizzly tracks. Decided I'd follow them. The tracks went up that northwest fork of the creek into all of that tag alder. They were on a game trail so I followed them. You know where I was just before you reach that steep pitch into the top basin. I looked up and couldn't believe my eyes. Looking at me was a grizzly bear. I shook my head and looked again. Now there was two heads looking at me. I backed up a step 'cause they weren't 50 feet from me, shook my head and looked again. Now there were four heads. Yes, four heads one on top of the other looking down at me. Only one head had a body."

"Did you get one?" I asked.

"Hell no. I looked at my old 30-30 and let those bear have that whole damn country. I feel like a man who has just lost his manhood."

Needless to say, Tom had done her right when he left. What really had happened was as he was climbing the last steep pitch up this hill on a bear trail through the tag alder and dwarf spruce, there were four bear coming down the trail and all each could do was rare up and look over the top of the bear in front of him.

That was Tom's last trip, but to this day, every hunter in the area calls this piece of country "Four Grizzly Gulch" and the grizzly are still there.

Grizzly country.

TED, THE HORSE TRADER

Ted was another character that worked for me. He was the best packer I have ever seen and could handle rough stock like nobody's business; the rougher the better for Ted. He was full of jokes. It never failed if things were really getting rough and tough, you could expect this Irishman to come up with, "Say did you ever hear about the guy..." and then he'd spin a yarn that would have everyone laughing and we'd forget our troubles.

He was always trading anything, but mostly horses. I'd be in need of some more stock and I'd call Ted and say, "Know where I can find this or that kind of a horse or mule?"

He'd say, "You bet. I'll be up with them in a few days." Or he'd say, "Come down and I'll show you some we can make a good deal on."

I always ended up with top stock at a reasonable price. Then he'd take my canners and trade them to someone else. He always had a deal going.

One day I called Ted up and said, "I've got these four saddle horses that are in good shape and gentle but just getting too many years on them. You know them." I tole him their names. He knew all my horses, had worked them all.

He said, "This a trade deal or you just want to sell them?"

I says, "I'd trade, but later on next spring. If you want to come get them before the next sale, OK, and come spring we'll do some trading."

Well, Old Ted come up the morning of the horse sale in Missoula and picks up these four old nags. On the way to the sale he passes a bar. Well, Ted don't pass up many bars. He stops and is having a drink or two when in walks Old Barney, who owns Holland Lake Lodge. He says to Ted, "Where you taking Howard's horses?"

Ted says, "To the sale ring. You need four good gentle horses?"

Barney says, "Why's he selling them? They're good and fat and they're good saddle horses. I've rode them."

Ted says, "I don't know. He just called me up and said he wanted to get rid of them."

Now old Barney is ripe for a deal and the wheels are spinning in Ted's head. He buys Barney a drink and says, "If you want them horses, I'll make you a deal you can't pass up. You got any old canners up at the lodge?"

Barney says, "I've got three or four but there're not that good."

Ted says, "Let's go look at them." So off to Holland Lake goes Ted and Barney.

Barney has a little single-footing horse, but about 33 years old. He's the smoothest thing you ever rode. Then three other old nags. Well, Ted finally talks Barney out of $175 boot and trades him horses. Old Ted stops at the bar again and stays there 'til it's too late to make the sale. Hap, who owns the bar, says, "What you going to do with them horses?"

Ted says, "I'll take them up and dump them in Howard's pasture 'til the next sale." And away he goes, heading for my place.

Well, along about midnight Marg says, "Ted's here. I can hear him laughing." About that time the back door flies open and it's Ted alright. He's about half lit and laughing his head off.

I says, "Wait 'til I get this coffee going and tell me what's so funny." Well, we got our coffee and Marg, Ted and me are setting around the kitchen table. Old Ted starts in and tells us about his deal with Barney. Then as he's coming up the road below my place he meets Tom, who owns the White Tail Ranch right next to our place. Tom stops him and says, "Where you going with the horses?"

Ted says, "I'm taking them up to Howard's."

Tom says, "Has he already bought them?"

Ted says, "He's never seen them."

Tom says, "How come you're always taking good horses to Howard and selling me some old canners?"

Ted says, "He pays me more money than you do."

Tom says, "Take them up to my place and we'll make a deal."

Ted says, "Fine." And up to White Tail he goes, laughing all the way.

Now Tom had just bought three three-year-old half Morgan and Thoroughbred colts for $250 around, but didn't have anyone to break them to ride.

Well, after Ted and him had bartered back and forth for a couple of hours, Tom says, "Are they gentle?"

Ted says, "Sure." He open the tailgate and unloads this little bay single-footing horse, jumps on him bareback with only the halter and rides him up and down the road. Now as he came by Helen, Tom's wife, he reaches down, picks her up on the horse. Ted slides off and Helen rides the horse down the road. When she comes back she says, "Tom I've got to have this horse. He's so smooth."

Well, Ted ends up trading all four of those old nags for the three colts plus another $175 and made a deal with Tom to keep the three colts for a month. Now Ted started out with four old canners worth $50 bucks apiece and ended up with three good young colts and $350 bucks to boot all in one day and had a party doing it.

I could write a book on his horse trading and trading for anything you can mention, even a gallon of paint on a billy goat. But that's another story.

Another time Ted was working for me and I had a very elderly gentleman on a special hunt. He wanted to get a bull elk on the bugle.

Now this old boy should have went on this kind of hunt 30 years before. He was not only too old, but in bad physical shape. One day I asked him why he never buttoned his fly on his pants. He says, "I can't. I've got arthritis in my hands so bad I can't pull the zipper." I said I'd do it for him.

Well, Ted traveled too fast for him, so I made a deal with Ted to cook and I'd guide the old boy. We traded jobs and the next morning me and hunter took off. We had not gone very far when a coyote shows up. He sets down on a hillside and is yapping at us as we rode by. I says, "You want to shoot that coyote?"

The old man says, "I sure would like to."

So I got him off his horse and all lined out. He let go and got the coyote dead center.

I told him to wait, I'd be right back. Then I rode over to the coyote and leaned down, picked him up and rode back to camp. I threw the coyote down in front of the cook tent and hollered at Ted, "When you've finished with your lady-like chores, skin this coyote out, Cookie," and rode off hunting again.

When me and my guest rode into camp that night, Old Ted hollers at me, "Hurry up. Supper is getting cold."

We went in to eat and sat down to steak, fried spuds and onions and canned corn. I really like steak and fried spuds and onions and this steak was done just right. Nice and tender.

Now the hunt proceeded and all went well. We finally got a fair bull and the Old Man back to the ranch and on his way home.

Now along the next spring I was going to the horse sale in Missoula. I needed to pick up some new stock for the summer. My son or daughter said, "Think you'll see Ted today?"

I said, "I probably will. He usually makes all the horse sales. Why?"

By this time they and my wife are laughing 'til they can't talk. I finally wormed it out of them what was so funny. Now this damn Ted had steaked and fed me and the hunter that cockeyed coyote. You couldn't beat that guy with a club.

We had this party of men who had become very close. They all met the first time in our hunting camp. After that they made it a special deal they would come hunting at the same time every year. You talk about a rough crowd. There was Ted, Chuck, Bud and Lewie, all of them rough and tough. They would hit each other as hard as they could, wrestle and roughhouse like a bunch of kids.

Me, I'm small, usually about 115 pounds. They would pick me up and throw me right out of the tent. Then sometimes pound on my arms 'til they were black and blue. Never a dull moment. I'd wait and pull any dirty trick I could on them. This went on for years.

Finally, one night Bud came into our bunk tent and says, "Ted you got anything that'll help hemorrhoids?"

Ted says, "No. I got some Vaseline that might make them slick and they won't hurt so much when you walk."

Well, this goes on for a couple of days. Bud is in bad shape. He can't walk, sit or anything without pain. In the middle of the night, in comes Bud. He's got a flashlight and a shaving mirror. He says, "Ted where is that Vaseline?" Ted digs into his war bag and gets the jar, takes off the cap and sets it on the floor.

Now I sleep right next to Ted and I get a tube of Ben Gay (hot rub) and squirt a big gob of it into the top of that Vaseline jar. Old Bud squats down with the mirror under him, dips his fingers in the Vaseline jar, picking up all this Ben Gay and he rubs it on his hemorrhoids.

What a squall! Bud flies out of that tent, jumps in the creek, squats down and splashes cold ice water on his hemorrhoids, hollering, "Oh! Oh! Oh!" I'm laughing with my head under my sleeping bag.

After a while, in comes Bud. Now he jumps on Ted, who is laughing, and pounds the tar out of him, Ted yelling, "I didn't know it would burn."

I never told a soul, just let it ride. Now I really felt good because I'd gotten even with both of them.

Now these hunts went on for four or five years. Every year Ted and Bud would do battle the first night they met. I'm really enjoying this. Both thought it was the Vaseline. By the way, it cured Bud's piles; he never had them again.

Finally, he called and wanted to go mountain lion hunting with me in the middle of the winter. We were way up on a steep mountainside. The snow was deep and we were on snowshoes. Well, I've worn snowshoes all my life but Bud is having trouble walking. We sat down under a tree to eat our lunch. Bud says, "You seen that damn Ted lately?"

I says, "Yeah, I see him off and on."

Bud says, "That dirty son of a buck and his Vaseline, I could kill him."

I started to laugh. He looked at me and says, "Why, you dirty rotten little weasel, you put something in that jar."

By now I was on my way down the hill. Poor old Bud jumps up and after me he comes. He makes about two jumps on those snowshoes and end over end he goes.

I says, "Well, I cured your piles for you."

Bud says, "Yes you did but every time I comb my hair they hurt."

Now Old Bud and his lovely wife were really my kind of people. Both Ted and Bud have made the big trip over the Big Divide, but I really miss them as if they left us yesterday.

SUCCESS

There is an old saying that "experience is the best teacher." Don't ever sell it short. What is learned by experience seldom leaves a man, especially when you hurt a little bit getting it.

We hired this lad, a mustanger from the Oregon and Nevada country. He had run mustangs and cattle from Battle Mountain, Nevada, up into the John Day country in Oregon, a big piece of landscape. He was an excellent horseman with ingenuity in his makeup. Jack could figure how to get a job done and do it, a top hand if there ever was one. He was a man to ride the trail with.

This outfitting was new to him and number one on his list was to shoot himself a nice bull elk. Jack bought himself an old 30.06 Springfield rifle, took a hacksaw and sawed the barrel off nice and short to fit well under his leg on a horse.

He was heading out to the ranch with a string of 10 pack animals loaded to the hilt. The trail led down the North Fork canyon. The North Fork River is a boiling white-water stream winding down a very narrow canyon, twisting and turning around the steep mountainsides, in some places a silver ribbon below the trail. Jack and his packstring are winding in and out as the trail goes. The trail crosses the top of a rock slide. Below the trail the slide runs down about 300 feet to a narrow flat along the river. Above is open timber, serviceberry and huckleberry bushes and red brush—good elk feed.

Now when Jack is out in the middle of the slide and his mules strung out behind him, he looks up the hill and there stands his elk. Like a flash, without a thought of the mules, he's off his horse and the old 30.06 barks. Down the hill rolls the elk right into the middle of his string. Now this elk had no brakes and cares less at this time. The impact rolls the whole string over the edge of the trail and head over heels down the rock slide coming to a rest on the little flat. This is what you call a wreck. What a mess!

Three hours later, after getting the mules on their feet, repacking them and dressing out the elk, he was back on the trail above. A very tired and proud guide rode into the ranch about 11:30 that night. He was wearing a sheepish smile and a gold star Mother Experience had given him.

Packing an elk back to camp.

42-SHOT BULL

When a hunter books with an outfitter he doesn't know if you are good or bad at the business unless he knows someone who has hunted with you. He has only your word over the phone or a letter that can be read many ways. By the same token, you as an outfitter are in the same spot. You don't know if you have booked a hunter or a bull artist. Big game hunters are notorious for telling big stories of shooting running game at 700 or 800 yards. An outfitter knows most game is taken standing at less than 100 yards. You only guess and hope this old boy can produce when the time comes right.

This particular hunter topped them all. He was very interesting to listen to. He claimed he never missed and had climbed all the peaks in British Columbia under rugged circumstances. Howie, his guide was about to throw in the sponge and forget him. The hunter couldn't do anything right. Howie said if you got him off the trail in the timber he'd fall over his own feet. He fell off his horse flat on his back one morning when they saw a bull while riding up the trail. Another time a bull was so close he couldn't have missed but he dropped his rifle and never got a shot. Now he still kept saying, "All I need is one decent shot. You just show me a bull."

He always carried two boxes of shells with him every day, and a loaded gun. This day Howie rode up on this ridge that looked into an alpine basin. The basin was void of trees except for little bunches here and there. Right in the creek having a drink were 10 cows and calves and one yearling spike. Better a spike than nothing, thinks Howie.

He gets his hunter set up and the shooting starts. Well, elk will get excited sometimes and just go around in a tight circle when they can't tell where the shooting is coming from. We call it milling. These elk did just this. This guy empties his gun, loads and empties it again. Finally, Howie is stuffing one shell in his gun at a time instead of a full load in hopes he'd connect before the elk took off. Finally, he shoots the right front foot off of this spike and the spike took off down the creek to the timber. By this time Mr. One Shot Hunter has shot 41 times. Howie grabs his hand gun, catches up to the bull in the edge of the timber and finishes him off.

Me and the other guides can hear all this shooting and we figure he's shooting at a rock or is having a little war all by himself.

When they rode into camp that afternoon, the cook says, "How many did you guys get anyway?"

Howie and his hunter are laughing, having a big time. Then Howie comes up with this lone, little elk foot and tells their story.

You never know about a guy, but you can usually guess.

Bear country in the Scapegoat Wilderness area.

THE BROWNSVILLE DRAWL

Funny things happen to funny people. Many years ago we booked a group of hunters from Brownsville, Texas. Now these boys really had a southern drawl. I've heard and talked and visited in the deep South, but these boys had a lingo all of their own.

One of them was a big, fat, redheaded guy who wore bib overalls of about one size too large. His shoes were special made for size and he'd have to stop every other step to let his shoes and overalls catch up. He'd never heard of the word "Quiet" and you couldn't get him close to a horse let alone an elk. The rest of the guides had given up on Big Red. Also, all his buddies were filled up on elk and just waiting for Red so they could go home.

I knew where there was an old, smart bull hiding out with his harem of cows. I could call him and he'd come just so far and then stand in this thicket racking his horns and bugling up a storm, but we couldn't get a look at him no matter how we tried.

We had just two more days to get Red to do his thing so I says to one of my guides, "Bill, you come with me this morning and we'll see if we can't do something for Red on that bull." Bill can handle a elk call pretty good and he knew just what to do.

Well, Red, Bill and I slip in right close and I gave Mr. Bull a toot. Right back he comes, so I says, "Bill, I'll keep him busy and you slip up closer. When you're set, give a bugle and I'll try to slip Red around and we'll come in the back door while you and the bull are bugling at one another."

After much slow maneuvering, I get behind the bull and sneak in close. It's a heavy big spruce swamp. Finally, real slow, I reach out and push a limb back for a look-see. Not 30 yards away is Mr. Bull looking in Bill's direction and raking his antlers on a tree. I says in a whisper, "Let him have it, Red."

In a big, deep Texas drawl, Red says, "Yassuh, Mr. Howard." You should have seen that bull go. His legs just disappeared. So did he, and straight ahead.

Then Bill's voice came loud and clear, "What the hell did you do to that bull?"

What happened was that Bill was squatted in a waterway right on the same game trail the bull was on. When Red spooked him, the elk took off in high gear straight at Bill. When he saw Bill, all the elk could do was jump, and jump he did, right over the top of poor Bill.

Early next morning I have Red on his horse and we're ready to go when along comes his buddy and wants to tag along. He's riding behind Red and Red right behind me. We are going up Spring Creek to the Rapid Creek Divide. When we get to the "Devil's Kitchen," a narrow rocky cut about 20 feet wide where we go along a rock ledge trail below a cliff, a tree has fallen across the trail just above my head. I stop, break all the branches off and you can just duck your head and ride under the tree. One limb sticks down lower than the rest but it's OK. I go under, and then tell Red to duck his head and come on.

When ole Red gets to the tree he just sort of nods his head and rides under. This long limb sticks through his wool shirt under his suspenders and he stops his horse, backs him up a bit, reaches up back and unhooks the limb, sits up straight and kicks Old Jim, his horse, in the ribs. Jim gives a big jump ahead, hooking the limb through the shirt again. Jim keeps coming but Red is hanging on the limb. He swings back and forth a couple of times like the pendulum on a clock, the limb breaks and Red falls to the rocky trail right on his face. I jump off my horse and run back to Red. He's out, cold as a cucumber. Finally we bring him to and he says, "Iz all right. Where's that bull?" So off we go again.

Coming out on a rocky point later that morning I get an answer to my bugle right below me in some dense fir on the Rapid Creek side. I know this bull is bedded at a wallow and I can't stalk him; I'll have to call him out. I pulled every trick I knew and he'd just lay there and bugle an answer to me.

Finally, I broke out my bones and started rattling them on the ground and an old log. This got him up and moving about. Suddenly I gave him a high pitched squeal and here he came right to us about 60 feet away. Red shot him dead center. Was I happy! Red and I walked down to the fallen bull. I said, "Red I'm going to eat my lunch before I dress and cape this bull."

We're eating our lunch, Red setting on the bull, when he says, "Yassuh, Mister Howard, the man who 'unts the bull helk without his whistle and bones, he's just dried up and blowed away."

Big Red went home happy with his elk and booming southern drawl.

JUST PLAIN GUTS

What makes great men and pushes them on beyond that point most people don't make in their lives? You can call it intestinal fortitude, ambition or personal desire. I call it guts. It makes them take that last long step into the impossible.

I booked this gentleman on a hunt in the late end of the season. It was after the bugle or rut season was over and we had snow. He told me he was crippled up and couldn't walk too good and he felt it was now or never if he was to fulfill his life-long desire to hang a trophy elk on his wall. I explained how difficult it would be at this time of the year. He almost begged me, saying, "I'll do my best if you'll do yours." I couldn't turn him down and hoped for the best.

When the time came for the hunt, my wife picked him up at the airport so when I came out of camp with the hunters he was waiting at the saddle shed when we rode in. I was shocked. This lad was really crippled up. He could hardly walk. I says, "Are you sure you want to do this?"

He says, "I've got to. I've waited all my life. In another year or two I can never do it."

The next morning, we and the rest of the party headed for camp 18 miles away. It was a tough, painful trip on him. Let's call him Jim. He told me he had a disease that dried up all the joint water in his body. When he bent his arm, his elbow sort of squeaked and if you laid your hand on his knees you could feel something like a squeak sound. I'm tellin' you, he was in pain everytime he moved. By the time we had reached camp, all of the other guests and my crew were sold on this guy. Every last one of them hoping he'd get his bull, even at their expense.

We hunted and hunted. Jim was riding Old Cotton, the horse, and me leading him, looking for a late season bull. An impossibility I was sure.

Finally, one day I was leading his horse up a game trail to some open sidehills where elk had been feeding quite regular throughout the season. All of a sudden from above and across a deep ravine comes this high, piercing bugle. I can't believe my ears. Then another long, drawn out elk bugle. I was completely surprised. The rut was over two weeks ago. Then from down below in a swampy area by the creek I hear this bull moose courting his cows, grunting and smashing the willows with his antlers. Silently I listen and soon I figured it out. There were two bull elk laying in the timber above, bugling at the moose in the creek. I watch and listen. Soon I have these two bulls located.

There is a deep wash that runs from the top of the ridge down to the swamp and creek. At the head end is a game trail crossing the wash and leading up a bank to a flat, timbered bench. It is here the elk like to bed during the day. To get there, I have to cross an open hillside for about 300 yards; then I can drop into the ravine out of sight of the bulls bedded on this bench. I've got to take a chance. So, leading Old Cotton and Jim, I eased around the hill slowly and made it to the wash, helped Jim off his horse and got his rifle hoping the bulls were still there.

I pushed Jim up the steep bank and he laid down in the game trail. I eased up beside him and gave him his rifle. We were resting when, right ahead and below, one bull bugled. I peeped over the huckleberry brush and 50 yards away lay two six-point bulls. I eased Jim to a sitting position and slipped him his rifle. As the bull jumped, the rifle cracked and down went the bull. I turned to Jim. He was laying flat on his stomach in the trail. He says, "I'm fine. Did I get him?"

I said, "Dead center." You should have seen the pleasure and contentment on his face.

Jim said, "Don't touch him. Let me rest." In a few minutes he was on his feet. I helped him to his elk and took pictures for him. While I caped and dressed the elk he laid down and never said a word, only looked and smiled.

When my job was finished, I went for Old Cotton, loaded Jim on and went to camp. That night after all the guides and hunters were back to camp there were toasts, made with more sincerity than I have witnessed before or since.

I received a note of appreciation but have never heard what happened to him. He surely left his mark on me. I'll never forget him.

DEMOCRATIC PERSONALITIES

While I'm on the character bit, I must tell you about some mules. Every mule has his own personality. Every one of them is a different stripe.

I had a mule I called Hungry by name. Now, if she knew you she was a real honey as a pack mule. But if a stranger come around, she'd act like a wild animal that had never seen a human before. She had this habit of when you'd meet some poor backpacker along the trail, old Hungry would come alive. The backpackers have a habit, it seems, of just stepping just far enough off the trail to let you slide by, almost bumping them. When you have 10 mules strung out behind you, you don't have much control over each one.

Well, old Hungry would hang back just as far as she could on her lead rope. When she got about even with the backpacker, she would give a big jump right at him and whistle like a bull elk. The poor lad standing there would dive for the brush, scared half to death. I never seen her hit one in her life, but she'd sure move them. Then she'd step back in line and you could almost see her grin.

One time we had a big fire up the North Fork and the Forest Service was walking the firefighters into the fire. Me and Ted were coming out with all 10 mules loaded heavy. Now right on a big rock slide I met these firefighters, about 150 or them. I asked them to step high off the trail so we could pass as we had some pretty rank mules in that string. Everybody climbed up the bank as we met them, giving us lots of room. There was one Negro in the bunch and when we came to him, he says to me, "I'ze alright, boss. I was born and raised with mules," and he just stepped off the lower side of the trail.

I said, "You better move farther away. You might get kicked."

He says, "I'ze all right. I can eat those long ears."

Well, I rode past and when Ted came up old Hungry hung back again. Now when she got even with that man, she made a dive at him and really whistled and snorted. Down over the hill went the man and all our young, rank mules blew up. We had packs under their bellies, some flat on their sides, just a real royal wreck.

Ted and me finally got them straightened out and started down the trail. Someone yelled at us from way up the hill in the rock slide. We looked up and sticking over a rock 50 yards up is this black face. He says,

Howard's caption for this photo reads: "The one with the hat is me."

"Boy, dem is really wild sons of _____."

Then there was Davie Crockett and Black Jack, two small black mules always right together. Real buddies.

When we were on summer trips and would lay over a day or two someplace, all the stock would be out grazing But not these two. They seemed to know when lunch time came. They'd eat anything from hot cakes to candy bars.

We usually set up a big kitchen fly with the stove in one end and along the side we'd have the cook table.

Now Davie Crockett would come up close to the kitchen with Black Jack right behind him. They would stand there letting on they were sound asleep. We'd take a loaf of bread, set it on the edge of the table with the open end pointed inward. Old Davie would take a sidestep closer to the fly, followed by Black Jack. They'd stop and stand with their eyes shut. Then another sidestep until they were about 3 feet from the table and loaf of bread.

They'd stand there as quiet as could be until you'd step away from your side of the table. Then, like a flash, Davie Crockett would grab the butt end of that bread and take off on a run, spilling the slices out the open end of the wrapper. Black Jack would run along behind with his nose on the ground and just like a vacuum cleaner pick up every slice of bread. Poor old Davie always ended up eating the bread wrapper and a couple of slices still in it. What a pair!

Another time the cook was cooking a big pot of oatmeal for breakfast. Well, old Davie wandered over by the cook shack and stood there, looking on. When the cook left the stove and turned his back mixing up some hotcakes, old Davie sneaked up, stuck his nose in that oatmeal and started eating that boiling mush. The cook turned and, seeing the mule eating his oatmeal, took after him cussing like a teamster late for dinner, waving the mixing spoon over his head, hotcake batter flying all over. Now it was cold and old Davie headed out with his head high and steam from the hot mush trailing back from his nose.

In a few days, poor old Davie Crockett's nose was all blistered and raw almost up to his eyes but it never stopped his raiding of camp if he got the chance.

I'm sure you can see why the Democrats use a mule for an emblem. You can't stop them, right or wrong.

Then there was Pinky. What a mule! He was another camp robber.

We were camped down on Limestone in the Danaher this evening with a large group of men. This particular evening, we were having T-bone steak with all the trimmings. Everyone got his plate of food and sat around wherever they found a log or block of wood, using their knees for a table.

On this trip was a gentleman, vice president of Chase Manhattan Bank in New York, who was a great story-teller and shooter of the bull. He and five or six other guys were seated in a half circle, sitting on some blocks of firewood.

Well, Bob got interested in telling this yarn, looking off to the left side at some of the boys. Old Pinky walked up behind him, reached over his shoulder and picked the T-bone off Bob's plate, backed up a step and proceeded to have himself a steak dinner. Now all the men were laughing at Pinky and Bob thought he'd told that story about right. He turned his head around and went after his steak. No steak. He looked around just as Pinky spit out the bone, well-cleaned. He jumped up and says, "Howard, how much for that mule?"

I says, "$1,000," still laughing.

He says, "I'll give you $1500 and you deliver him to my home in New York."

I says, "A deal." Pinky lives in New York now and has never worked a day in his life since.

Old Mose.

JUST A BABY

One year I received this phone call from a doctor way down in Raleigh, North Carolina, and he just had to go elk hunting. We talked for a long time. He told of whitetail deer hunts, of the big heads he'd taken all the way from Texas up and along the East Coast to upstate New York and the great deer country of Pennsylvania.

There was no talking him out of it. He just had to have a Boone and Crockett bull elk and would settle for nothing else. I told him you did not just hunt and get a trophy head like that anywhere in 10 days except by chance and good luck.

Well, we never got together on a hunt, but he'd call every once in a while and talk elk hunting. I told him he'd better try some other outfitter. He just sounded like trouble to me.

Now this went on for several years. Finally, we got together on this hunt. I told him I could guarantee nothing but to cash his check as soon as I got it and do my best for him.

Doc finally arrives rarin' to shoot an elk. He was a little man, very excitable and always dressed like he'd just stepped out of a fashion show. He still was going to shoot nothing but this Boone and Crockett head.

The first morning in camp, Doc and I head up the mountain, tied our horses in a protected spot and took off on foot. After hunting for an hour or so, climbing pretty good, I sat down for a breather.

Just for fun I gave a bugle and right back comes a challenge. The elk was off to our left on some lodgepole benches. After them we go.

The closer we got the more this old boy would bugle. Suddenly I realized it was not just one bull but three or four and I had them spotted. They were in a ravine where a big spring came out of the side of the mountain. Right above us was a big game trail that would take us right to that spring.

Well, we climbed up to the trail and being rainy weather it was real quiet traveling. When we came to the edge of the ravine, I peeked over and a spike was having a drink at this spring. I squatted down and turned to my hunter. Doc sees the spike and threw his rifle up to shoot. I grabbed his gun and says, "No. That's just a spike." Boy did he get mad. I said, "You want a big bull. You're not going to shoot 'til we see at least a decent one."

We sat there 'til our spike finished his drink and he trotted on around the hill to catch up to the rest of the elk. Then I says, "Come."

We slipped down that trail right past the spring and around the hillside. Before I knew it, I found we were right in the middle of about 25 head of elk. We squatted down right in the trail by a big fir tree.

I got Doc all ready and then let go a bugle. Right back comes an answer. He's not 50 yards ahead and below a bit. Then came a big, hoarse bugle to my right and above and behind, real close. What to do now! While I'm trying to decide, another elk bugled farther ahead of us. I give another blast on my bugle. Right in front and below comes this bugle from the number one elk. You can almost feel the hot breath.

Then I see the yellow sides of a bull stepping through the branches of a big, heavy spruce tree. He's going to come right out on the game trail. I show him to Doc and whisper, "Don't shoot 'til I tell you because the old herd bull is right above us."

This big herd bull is a dandy. He is coming at a trot down the sidehill at the same time the number one bull steps around that tree. He's a small six-point. I says, "Don't shoot."

Ker-Bang! Doc shoots anyway. The bull falls, jumps up and heads for parts unknown.

I says, "Doc, why'd you shoot? He's just a baby. The old herd bull was coming right down to the trail."

Doc says, "Maybe he's a baby to you but to me he's the grandest bull on earth and I've only got a nursery to hang his head in."

Well I trailed the bull for 100 or 150 yards around the trail and found him in a pile. He was a beautiful symmetrical head, but small.

Doc never went hunting for elk again. I talked to him not too long ago and he is still very pleased with his bull.

This is one reason when people ask me what is a trophy elk, I can honestly say I don't know except that the trophy is only seen by the eyes of the beholder.

MY FRIEND LARRY

This is a conglomeration of tales in a way of a tribute to one of my best friends. He is a writer, hunter, story-teller and sportsman; in other words, one of the grandest guys ever to hunt this great country of ours.

I will call him by his first name and anything I say is with respect, nothing else, be it good or bad.

Another guy who accompanied us on every hunt over many years was Bill, a photographer and writer in his own realm. He'll surely come up in these little stories.

I remember the first hunt as if it was yesterday. Larry and Bill had an assignment from a sporting magazine to do a feature article and get a cover picture for their hunting issue. What was wanted was a shot of Larry shooting a goat or elk, all in the same picture. Quite a job!

Well, we spotted this old billy goat high up in a ravine on the Calf Creek cliffs. We made the climb, got above him and found a goat trail that led us right into position. Remember, we are on a goat trail about 10 inches wide on the side of a cliff. You can look straight down for 300 feet and then on down a steep mountainside for a mile. Lots of scenery. Bill's got the big box camera, me the tripod and film.

This goat trail ran along the cliff in and out of ravines and washes for about three-quarters of a mile. It was not easy to follow or negotiate. At some places it was only four or five inches wide and we'd have to hang on to outcropping rocks and scrub brush to get around some points of the cliff. And at some places I'd have to help them slide into a ravine or climb back out. All the time we had 300 to 400 feet of open space below us. Lots of rocks and treetops down there but no hand holts in between. Just air. Lots of it.

We came around one of these tough points and right in front of us and below in a wide wash is Mr. Billy. He's grazing on some lichen plants right in the middle of a green spot. The sun is shining on him and his dinner table, a beautiful picture. We're in a tough spot, no wide goat trail and very little brush to use as a rough-lock. It's now or never. We've got to set up here and hope we don't spook him.

I get Larry all lined up and then get Bill set up with the black sack over his head and tell him, "When you're ready, wiggle your toe and I'll tell Larry to shoot. Mr. Billy Goat is still grazing about 35 yards away. He

The Kollar party poses with their guides and the camp cook.

hasn't spotted us yet.

In his excitement, Bill forgot that his heel hooked into a crevice in the rock was his only support on the cliff. He wagged his toe too far, Larry shoots and Bill and the camera crash down past him. Larry grabs the camera tripod, I grab and get Bill by the belt. Bill still has hold of his camera. We're all there dangling over the edge of the goat trail and a 300 foot fall. I have a death grip with one arm and a leg around a dwarf juniper. With much ado and lots of pulling, we scrambled back on the ledge.

My heart was right out in the open. Such a narrow escape. Then Larry's voice, "Did you get the picture? You know there's an extra $2,000 bonus to be split, don'tcha!"

Now I had done my part and Larry had done his, getting a 10 3/4 inch billy, but Bill didn't do so well. When Bill hit his darkroom and processed the film, did he have a picture? It was beautiful scenery of the bottom of that cliff and all the Danaher Meadows far below, but no Larry and no

Larry Koller and goat.

goat.

From then on for many years when we'd get together, whether on a hunt or at a bar, it always turned out the same—Bill claiming Larry pushed him and Larry expounding on the awkwardness of a damn photographer he knew.

Another time it was dry and hot in early September with no thought of rain or snow. We were after the granddaddy of them all. Larry just had to have a big bull elk to prove out this hunt he was writing up.

Early one morning I picked up a real old, hoarse bugle and hoping it to be an old boy, we started our stalk. Well, it had us up Hay Creek into a heavy stand of lodgepole so thick you could see only about 50 yards or less. This bull would answer my call every time and challenge me as hot and heavy as I've ever heard, but he would not move from his bed.

I says, "Larry, we got to go after him. We've got to be quiet. You only move when I do, right together. We've got to make him think it's another bull sneaking in." So away we go. After what seems like hours of one step at a time, he bugles right in front of me. Mebby 20 yards. I looked but couldn't spot him. All of a sudden, out of the beargrass rises this big old monarch. What a sight! Larry stands there like a statue. Didn't even raise his gun. After what seemed like hours, Mr. Bull explodes, knocking saplings this way and that. Now Larry explodes and Ker-Pow, away goes the bull as the timber closes behind him.

"Did I hit him?" says Larry.

"No," I says.

"Yes, I did," says he. Well, we followed him as best we could for a half a mile or so and then lost his tracks. Still no blood. "I'll never shoot at an animal again when I'm that excited," says Larry, "I might of wounded him."

Later that afternoon I caught another bugle, got in close and started my serenade. Lo and behold, right back came several answers. I bugled a few more times and raked a tree with a bone and out come number one bull into a little clearing, a nice respectable bull. Larry's all ready to shoot when out comes another from the other side. Now what? They start to spar around in that grassy arena causing all kinds of noise. Then comes the big herd bull neck bowed bugling and grunting, saliva dripping from his open mouth. He shags the other younger bulls around the little park and off into the thicket.

I says, "Why the hell didn't you shoot?"

Larry politely says, "Old Friend, I told you this morning I'd never shoot at any game again if I became that excited. Now I find that I wasn't even excited in my whole life 'til right now."

The next morning, Larry filled his tag with a nice bull. Whether he ever wrote of this hunt I'll never know, but I'm sure he lived it again and again until he was called away to the Happy Hunting Grounds.

CALF CREEK BULL

Another of these hunts with Larry proved to be very successful timing and funny.

In the party was a fellow called Vic. Now Vic was a small man, very short, plump and dressy. He always looked like he was ready for a formal party where he was to deliver a speech. He was a very excitable little Italian, a perfectionist at all times. Also very slow.

After many unsuccessful days of hunting, it became my luck to try and get Vic his trophy. Well after much ado and grand preparation we started out on our day's hunt. Not knowing where I could go to help the situation, I just let my horse move along. He turned up Calf Creek and I decided we'd try for the Calf Creek Bull. This was one of those old Mossyhorns that had got big and old only because he was smart. He had a hideout under the Calf Creek cliffs in a dense thicket of second growth fir.

However, as we rode along all of a sudden he bugled up ridge from us. We had ridden right between him and his hideout. I quickly hid the horses and hustled Vic up a little rocky ridge where we had good view of his path to and from.

I bugled and back he came, challenging whoever crossed his path looking for a chance at his cows. First came the cows and calves right past us, and then this big old boy pushing them along and challenging anyone to give him a try. By the time the cows had gone by us, Vic was almost uncontrollable. Then, up walks the Calf Creek Bull, six points on one side and seven points on the other, real heavy of beam and lots of spread.

I says. "Let him have it." He was about 20 feet from our hiding spot. You could see him from hoof to top of his antlers, no brush, trees or grass.

Vic just sat there looking through his sight. I reached over and hit him. He was like a rock. I hit him again and he came alive. Four times he shot. With the fourth shot, the bull threw his head in the air and I could see he was shot through the nose. Quickly, I unlimbered my handgun and administered the coup de grace.

Vic jumped up and ran to my side as I stood over the bull. He slaps me on the back and says, "Howard, I run one of the fanciest and finest drink and dine spots in upstate New York. You know I never saw that bull's body 'til right now. God, he's big."

I says, "Vic, if you never saw this bull, what the hell was you shooting at?"

He calmly replied, "All I could see was that magnificent head and horns over my backbar and I guess I shot right between them."

Thank God Vic was a notoriously poor shot.

My friend, Larry, was the top sportswriter of the 40's, 50's and 60's, being an ardent sportsman who hunted the whole of the North American continent as Outdoor Editor for *Argosy* magazine and the author of his many gun books and journals. He always brought a fine group of his close friends to help him enjoy the hunt and he never pushed himself into first place. He insisted on giving others first place whether it was at the bar or on the mountain shooting an elk.

I have been a lot of different places and talked with sportsmen in the hunting circles throughout the United States and Larry Koller's word on guns and hunting carry as much respect as the man himself.

Thank you, Larry.

Steve Copenhaver bringing a bull in that was taken in real elk country.

WALSH PARTY

After a letter or two over a few months, I get a phone call from a client. He and two other men want to book a goat only hunt for the following season.

Now, this is great, but he only wants one hunting license and wants to hunt nothing but a goat. His two friends are observers only. He's happy with paying full for all three of them, so this is good. Me and Gene, my brother, can handle them without help and Wendell and the other guides can handle the regular elk camp.

Now the day came and our guests arrive. One is an old man in his late 70's and the others are both doctors and young.

The next morning when we are making up the packs, here they come with their duffle. Boy, was it big, heavy and lots of it. We packed it up and lit out. We made our halfway camp in good shape, but a concerning thing was that Tom, the elderly gentleman, did not come to supper. The Doc said he was just tired.

Our goat camp was up Cabin Creek on the side of Scapegoat Mountain at about 8,000 feet. We were at our main hunting camp at 6,000 feet. When we started to pack up next morning, we suggested they leave all things not needed at base camp and only take enough stuff for overnight. But no deal. They had to take all their duffle. So what... It was only nine miles to goat camp.

We were camped in a meadow right at the foot of the last high ridge that formed the lower edge of this big basin on the top of the mountain we wanted to hunt. Scapegoat Mountain is a big, open, rocky mountain with lots of limestone cliffs and many wet cirques filled with succulent plants goat love to eat. It is the best goat country in Montana.

When we arrived at camp early in the afternoon, I was preparing supper when Gene says, "While you're getting something to eat, I'll run up on the bench and see if I can spot a good billy."

"OK," says I and away he goes.

He comes flying back in a few minutes and says, "There is about 30 head up there and a couple of good billies."

I dropped my supper, we got our hunter and says, "Let's go."

Now, from where we were camped to the bench and the goats it's not over 200 yards but pretty steep uphill on the main trail. Out of the bunk

Wendell Copenhaver with a Danaher Mountain billy.

tent comes our hunter and the two doctors. The doctors are carrying these two huge backpacks. They give one to Gene and one to me. "What's this junk?" I says.

"Oxygen bottle, hose, masks and medication," says Dr. Gray. Then we realize Tom is in really bad shape. Something's wrong.

Well, up the hill we start. All of a sudden, down falls Tom. The doctors grab our packs. Out come oxygen, masks, etc. They slap them on Tom and turn on the valves. Right away, Tom is ready to go again. Now this happened four times before we could peek over the rim into the rocky basin, but there stands Mr. Billy on a ledge all by himself. Gene got Tom into position and KerBoom, he's got his goat.

Gene says, "I'll skin the goat. You pack up and head for camp. We've got to get these guys out of this altitude."

"OK," says I.

When we got to camp, I put all three of them on their saddle horses and started them down the trail to the main camp. Then, I packed up their duffle, etc., loaded the mules and Gene and me caught them before they reached camp. The next morning, we loaded up and went out to the ranch.

Now I was a bit out of sorts at a man who would book a very strenuous hunt knowing he might drop dead at any minute and not tell his outfitter, so I jumped the Old Boy and told him how I felt.

His answer to me was, "If I had told you what shape I was in, you

Howard carrying the cape from Billy Lyons big billy taken on Danaher Mountain.

wouldn't have booked me. Now will you do me a last big favor?"

I said, "Yes." Then he gave me the cash price of having his billy mounted. Also, he gave me $100 bill to give the taxidermist to drop things and do his. Now $100 then was like $500 today.

In record time, the billy was done and shipped to Tom. Nothing more was heard for a long time. Then one day I got a hand-written letter from one of the doctors, thanking us for giving them a trip they really enjoyed. Then he went on to tell about Old Tom.

Well, Tom had hunted all over the world. He had a grand slam on sheep, lion, tiger, elephant, jaguar, etc., from all over the world, but no mountain goat. He had reserved a spot on the wall in his North American Trophy Room for the day when he got his billy.

Over the years, Tom had contracted leukemia and also bone cancer, along with about everything that could go wrong with his heart. Bill and Carl were his personal doctors and they went with him everywhere in his last years.

When his billy arrived, the three of them hung his head in the space on the wall. Tom sat in an easy chair admiring the trophy. Bill and Carl went into the bar and mixed a toddy to drink to the goat on the wall. When they returned to the trophy room, Old Tom, with a smile on his face, sat dead in the chair, the end of a life-long dream.

This makes you feel real good when you have helped someone gain a successful ending to such a dream. It's what keeps you going when you want to quit, just to be a part of fulfilling another's life.

A hunting camp on the Dry Fork.

EXCITEMENT OF THE HUNT

Wherever you are or whenever it may be and you are talking big game hunting, the old saying "buck fever" will come up.

Now people hunting wild game can become so excited they'll do many silly things. In hunting elk, just listening to a bull bugle excites me still and I have heard them all of my life. When you set waiting for a bull to appear and he is thrashing the brush with his antlers, pawing the ground and bugling so close to you that you can almost feel his breath and still can't see him, and if the wind is right you can smell his musky odor, don't tell me you're not going to be excited. Just to see a big monarch will do it. This is what makes hunters hunt. When the excitement wanes, the hunter dies.

Dan was guiding this fellow, Larry. Now Larry and Dan had hunted together for three years before this special hunt.

Now Larry is a whitetail deer hunter. I don't think even he knows how many he has taken in his home state of Pennsylvania. He is considered an expert shot with a rifle, both fast and deadly.

The first year Dan, the guide, and him were hunting up on old Whiskey Ridge when Dan spotted three good mulie bucks. He slips in right close and old Larry limbers up and misses both of them. A few days later, Dan calls up a big five-point bull mebby 25 to 30 yards. And again Larry misses, slick as a whistle. Larry is fit to be tied.

Now Dan has about had it and Larry can't believe his rifle is shooting right, so he takes another and they head for Lake Mountain. They pick up some bugling, but no luck. The next day they try another piece of country and Larry misses a real trophy buck. He comes to camp walking on his chin. He's really down in the dumps.

A couple of days later they try Lake Mountain again. A bull is bugling and they slip in and spot him about 300 yards off on an open sidehill. Larry gets all set up with a rest and settles down and misses again. That same evening they call up another bull and have the same luck. Now this is four bulls and three big bucks Larry's missed at different ranges and he's had it and is really disappointed. He just can't understand how he could miss.

"I'll be back," he says when he left for home. Of course, by now everyone in camp is on him and all six hunters are from his hometown so he can't build any stories to tell the folks back home. He's in for a rough bout at deer camp this fall.

Along about mid-November I gets a call. It's Larry. He says, "You know what, Howard? The first day of the deer season I saw a buck running across a field about 350 yards away and I leveled him with one shot, a real big 15-pointer. I want to book for next year. I want a bull elk."

I says, "OK. S'pose you want a new guide."

He says, "I want Dan. Me and him understand each other."

I says, "OK." And Steve books him and three of his buddies.

The next year was almost a repeat of the first. He missed both bucks and bulls but only three this year and he loudly proclaims never to hunt elk again, "Even if I am getting better at this mountain climbing."

Steve and I are visiting some of our hunters that winter in Pennsylvania. When we see Larry, he says, "You've got to see my new gun. I'm going to prove it to them damn elk that I can shoot." We had lunch with him and his wife and he hauls out this new rifle. It's a 338 Browning bolt action. Now this is really a solidly built firearm, and good.

Well, when the boys arrive he and Dan head for Cabin Creek, pick up this bugle and work in on this bull and his cows. After several hours of bugling and crashing brush, this old monarch shows himself about 300 yards off. There is no way to get closer and it's getting late, so they decide to try from where they're at. It's a standing shot and good and open. Larry gets set and lets him have it. Miss again. Larry jerks the bolt back and strips it right out of the gun, plumb ruined the gun.

When they got to camp, both were batting zero. I finally talked Larry into taking our old Model 70-338 and forget it.

The next evening, in come Dan and Larry just like a couple of teenagers at a party. Larry had got a real big, heavy six-pointer and healed all previous wounds.

Those big bulls and their bugling sure keyed him up. It's what makes the hunt worthwhile I guess.

A DOCTOR IN CAMP

On one trip I can remember so well my top guide, Tim by name, had filled his two hunters with elk and was raring to go goat hunting with one of them who had a license and really had to have a billy. I usually guided goat hunters myself as I knew where the billies hung out. But mostly I loved to hunt goat.

I do not believe in shooting a nanny due to the slowness of a mountain goat's natural reproduction. It's hard for some people to distinguish a large nanny from a young billy. I cautioned Tim and the hunter both and directed Tim to where I knew a billy was ranging up on Apex Mountain, a high limestone peak with lots of caves that goat use for protection and to hide in.

Along about 10 o'clock Tim spots the Billy. The stalk was made and the hunter misplaced his shot, wounding the goat. Well, Tim went after him. It entailed some very rough rock work and it was pretty iced up up there in the cliffs. Mr. Billy went around a ledge and into a cave. Right after him goes Tim. Inside, the cave opens out into a very large room but pretty dark. Tim strikes some matches and spots blood on a shelf-like trail leading up the wall of the cave to another opening. Tim thinks, "I'll crawl up and goose him out so Hank, who was waiting outside, can finish him." Well, up goes Tim but down comes the goat real mad to think Ole Tim is invading his domicile. Just in time, Tim sees the predicament he's in and jumps for the floor of the cave. At the same time his 44 Mag roars. Luckily, he killed the goat but him and the goat landed in the same pile.

Thanking his lucky stars, Tim drags the goat to the ledge at the mouth of the cave for light. Tim gets busy dressing and skinning the goat. The ledge is awful steep and icy. All of a sudden, the goat starts to slide out of the cave and over the edge into nothing. Tim grabbed for the goat and also slipped, but he caught himself. In doin' so he slashed his right shin with his knife, gashing it about eight inches long clear to the bone. Now he's nine miles from camp and first aid. With a couple of bandaids and a dirty handkerchief he bound his leg, finished skinning the goat, picked up the Billy, joined his hunter and headed for camp.

Along about 10:30 that night, in hobbles Tim and Hank, very jubilant. When I saw the blood, I says, "Let me see that leg." Tim jerked off his pants. What a leg, swollen, dirty and sore. I started washing it with soap and water and a disinfectant. Every time I touched it, old Tim would cuss me and wince with pain. I said to my son, Steve, "Go get me that fifth of bourbon." Steve hands it to me and I says, "Take a big jolt, Tim, and I'll be done in a minute." Well, he takes a big snort and hands me the bottle. I tips that jug up and washes that cut with it. You never heard such profanity in all your born days and it was every bit directed at me.

Tim went out to a doctor in a day or so when the swelling went down. The doctor says, "What did he use for disinfectant?"

Tim says, "A fifth of whiskey."

The doctor says, "Couldn't have used anything better but it sure is a waste of good whiskey."

Tim has never asked me to patch him up since.

The author plying his skill as a back country cook.

SLEEPING SICKNESS

An outfitter's job sounds like all fun and no work, pretty glamorous. Believe me there is more to it than riding a horse up the trail. You have to be some sort of a medic for both people and horses and mules, a cook, horseshoer and diplomat. Every once in a while you lose some hide or break a bone or two. Talking about people getting hurt in this business, well it doesn't happen very often but one must always be on his toes to prevent it.

One year sleeping sickness was going around the country and we decided to vaccinate all our stock before it stopped at our door. We had 120-some horses and mules. Now this is quite a job but it's got to be done. In innoculating for sleeping sickness, you must place your needle between the outer and inner layers of skin. It's sort of a ticklish deal and you must have the animal laying or standing quiet.

We had hired a Texas lad and his wife to work at the ranch that summer. He was (he claimed) a top college rodeo rider from some Ag college in Texas. I told him to be on hand early, meaning 6:30 or 7:00 in the morning, to help Steve, Howie and me with this job.

Finally, about 10 o'clock our college boy showed up. The best he could do was hand Howie the needles after Steve had filled the syringe. He was all decked out in his cowboy best, green and white chaps and all. However, he wouldn't get in the corral. He was either afraid he'd scare the stock or get those pretty chaps dirty.

I would forefoot the rank stock and then Howie would grab holt and help me throw them. When they hit the ground, I'd jump on their head and ear them. Howie'd shoot the needle to them and then we'd get another.

Finally, we got down to the last one, a real snaky thoroughbred three-year-old colt. We dumped him and needled him. Howie says, "Let him go." I turned loose of his head and threw off the foot rope. This colt scrambled up. As he did he stuck his head through the loop on the ground. Howie and I saw what had happened and both grabbed the rope and popped the colt around to face us. I made a quick grab for the rope to throw the loop off his head. The colt was quicker. He wheeled and kicked me right in the chest. I flew back, hitting Howie's head with mine—knocked Howie clear out of the corral and me clear out, period.

When I came to a bit and the clouds faded, I looked right into the whitest face and biggest eyes I've ever seen—Tex, with his head sticking through the corral fence. Suddenly I realized Steve and Howie were trying to get me up. I say, "Leave me lay 'til I see if I got a punctured lung. I think my ribs are busted." As I said the corral was real sloppy, about six inches deep. Those boys took me at my word and dropped me right back in that soup. It ran in my ears and down the back of my shirt. The white face of our Texas cowboy and the return to the corral mud was too much for me and Howie both—we started to laugh and couldn't stop. Old Tex took one more look, dropped the pack of needles and was gone.

The boys helped me up to the house to get cleaned up and head to town to see the doctor. Our college cowboy and wife and all their gear passed us. Where he was headed I don't know. He didn't even stop for his last week's wages. We've never heard of him since.

Mebby it looked a bit rough or he just couldn't take our insane laughter, damned if I know which.

When the doctors finished with me and Howie, I had seven broken ribs and 11 stitches in the back of my head where my head had hit Howie in the forehead. Howie had 29 stitches in his forehead, proving how hard-headed I am.

Back at camp the hunters display their hunt's trophies.

A FIGHT 'TIL DEATH

Many's the great bull that my guests have taken with broken antlers or sores of unhealed abscesses due to the fight for supremacy and the right to sire his harem.

One time I bugled a bull out of his harem but he would only come to the edge of a thicket that hid his lady friends. Here he would keep himself concealed, bugle and rake the trees. Rory, my guest, and I sat there bugling, rubbing a tree with a bone. I was using all the elk talk I knew to bring him out of the thicket. We could see the trees wave as he raked them with his antlers and we got a glance of his yellow body through the limbs every once in a while. Rory kept his sights on the spot 'til I thought he'd never hit him when he did show.

Finally he stepped out of the brush, giving Rory a clear shot and we had our trophy. When we went to dress him out we found he was really beat up from a fight with another bull. One shoulder was broken and his ribs punctured. His off-side ham was punctured in two different places. Both wounds were infected and an abscess about the size of a basketball hung out on his flank and ham. This bull walked on three legs. Now this bull was still in charge of nine cows and ready to do battle again. Remember, he had a broken front leg and was so infected we could not use the meat and still Mother Nature called upon him to challenge all comers and sire his cows. Mother Nature's a tough old girl.

It made me and my guest stand and wonder how many men would do the same, or if we could show such courage under like circumstances.

A few years back I was guiding a fellow who wanted a mountain goat and a bull elk. Well, we set out to get the billy first. After some climbing and spotting, we found this big old fellow up on Apex Mountain. We made a stalk and slipped up on him just as he went into a big cave to bed for the day. I says to my hunter, "Let's just park here and along about 4 o'clock Mr. Billy will come out to feed and we'll be in just the right spot." We are on a rocky ridge where we can look over a lot of prime elk country. Below us is a little dry lake bed with second growth all around it. Along about 2 o'clock a bull bugled below the lake. I answered him and right back came four or five more bugles, all close but scattered all around the lake in small dense timber. I gave them the old come-on again, raking a tree with a stick. The first thing we knew we'd stirred up a regular sym-

Bull elk.

phony of bull elk bugles. It seemed like each one was trying to outdo the other. At last the old herd bull, a big six-pointer, walked out on the lake bed about 60 yards below us. My guest was getting a line on him when out comes another big old boy. I said, "Hold it," to my hunter. "Let's see which has the best head." About that time the number one bull makes a rush at his friend and the fight was on.

You can't imagine such a conflict. They would rush each other, ram and push one another from one side of the lake bed to the other, with strips of hair and meat flying and dangling from those ivory-pointed antlers. We sat spellbound, not saying a word, as we watched. Then out of the brush came the cows. They ringed the edge of the lake and watched the battle. The small bulls stood off a ways on their own point, bugling their heads off.

Finally, one bull upset the other against a down log. He kept ramming him in the side with those great tines 'til the bull tried to get up no more. Then the victor rammed his antlers into the side of vanquished bull and threw him like a bale of hay over his back. Then he wheeled and did the same thing over again.

My guest says, "Howard, I came out here for a trophy and that dead bull is what I want."

I says, "Let's go down and run that bull away and cape him out." We stood up and started down to the battlefield. All the elk took off except for the big bull. He defied us in every way to come any closer. Finally, we threw rocks and sticks and he reluctantly moved up the ridge. When he topped the ridge skyline he stopped, looked back and bugled his defiance to all that could hear. My guest says, "Do you know what?" Then it hit me. We had watched this giant battle with each of us carrying in our backpack a 16mm movie Kline Kodak, one outfitted with a telephoto lens, and we had not taken one picture or even given it a thought.

I would bet my money the next bull that challenged this champ would really have a round for himself.

We dressed the elk out and climbed back up on that rocky ridge to look for our goat. Along about 5 o'clock out of the cave came our goat. Mr. Billy feeds around a game trail right to us. When he got to about 100 yards distance, my guest got him, a real nice trophy with 10 1/2 inch spikes. We skinned him and headed for camp. What a day! We have a good six-point bull, a beautiful billy trophy and a great story to tell our unbelieving friends at camp.

When we sat down to supper and started to tell our story, everyone started to laugh. Then my brother says, "We already heard all about it."

I says, "What do you mean!" Well, it seems that Bill, the new game warden, had followed me that day. He said he had to learn what kind of a outfitter I was. Now Bill is part Indian and he pulled a sneak on me and watched the whole thing from the rocks right above us. I didn't know he was in the country.

I have seen elk spar and run one another off but nothing like these two bulls. In all my hunting experiences I have found only three other dead bulls that showed they were killed in a fight. Don't ever let anyone tell you that man is the only animal that kills another in a fit of jealousy.

A Pennsylvania hunter with a trophy mule deer. The same hunter also took a nice bull elk while hunting in the Scapegoat Wilderness.

THANKS FOR BUTTING IN

It's not all as tough being a game warden as it sometimes sounds, if by chance you have a good personality and can enjoy a joke that's played on you. I have a friend who can enjoy things at his own expense and loves to tell others of the plights he has gotten himself into from time to time. I wish I could relate this incident with the enthusiasm and gusto Jack could.

Jack was a game warden over on the Fort Peck area for a number of years and became well acquainted with everyone in the vicinity. This area has a permit system of licensing and you can draw either a cow or a bull permit, if you are lucky. Very few permits are given out.

On the first day of the season, Jack is sitting up on a ridge where he can get a good view of the surrounding area with his binoculars when all of a sudden he spots a hunter making a sneak on cow elk. Watching this operation with much interest, he finally sees the man shoot the cow. Now, after shooting the cow, Mr. Hunter turns around and walks back up the hill, never even going to the elk he had just shot. After an hour or so Jack decides he had better go over and see what's going on.

After another 45 minutes Jack arrives at the scene of the kill. Still, there is no hunter anywhere so Jack dresses the elk and drags it down to an old road figuring he'll drive his pickup around and load the elk.

Just as he gets to the road, around the corner comes the hunter in his pickup. He gets out and Jack says, "Are you the guy that shot this cow?"

The hunter says, "Yes I did."

Jack says, "How come you didn't come down and dress it out?"

The hunter says, "Well, my pickup was up on top of the mountain and I figured I'd save myself some footwork by going up to the pickup and driving around and down here."

Jack says, "That's smart. I'll help you load it." After the elk was loaded Jack, being a good guy, says, "You better put your cow permit on her."

The guy says, "I don't have a cow permit."

Jack says, "Well in that case I'll have to arrest you and confiscate the elk. Put your bull permit on it and I'll punch it illegal. Since it's on your pickup, you can drop it off at the freezer plant for illegal game in Broadus."

The guy says, "I don't have a bull permit."

Jack again, "You don't have a bull permit? Well, put your regular hunting license on it."

Hunter again, "I don't have a hunting license."

By this time Jack has about had it and he says, "If you don't have a cow permit and no bull permit and not even a hunting license, just what the hell are you trying to do?"

The hunter says, "You damn fool, I was trying to poach an elk until some dumb game warden butted in."

Looking up the right hand fork of Dry Fork, deep in the wilderness.

THE MEXICAN

My son, Steve, by this time has become an accomplished guide himself. He had ridden these trails, followed me and watched how my guides and I worked. His first trip was a summer packtrip when he was six years old. Experience is a good teacher and he was a good student; he did not miss much.

He finished school and we formed a partnership. In later years he bought out my interest. Today he is a top outfitter with lots of experience behind him, tough, conscientious and a good hard hunter—hunts both early and late as you will see.

This is a story about some Mexican hunters from Mexico City.

Every hunter I've had from Mexico has been an excellent shot, the quietest and some of the best hunters I have probably had from any one area. I think the reason for this is that Mexicans are either very poor or comfortably fixed with the pesos. These hunters I have had train for a month or more before a hunt, testing themselves for stamina and going without water for a long time. They also run, stop and shoot at rocks, etc. They live at a high altitude and hunt desert mule deer that are up at 10,000 to 12,000 feet. It is very dry and tracking them is very difficult in the sand and rocks. Tough terrain makes a good hunter.

On this hunt one fellow was packing an Army Springfield with open sights and a .06 caliber. Steve was guiding him. One day they came out on a hillside and, looking across a long open ridge, they spied a large bunch of elk. Steve glassed them and said to Jose, "There are four bulls in that bunch but they're all small. There is one five-point that's not too bad, but he's small."

Jose asked, "How far away is he and which one is best?"

Steve showed him the bull and said, "That one laying out by himself on the right. He's 375 to 400 yards away."

Jose asked, "Can you make them run?"

Steve says, "Sure, why?"

Jose says, "Well, I came all the way from Mexico City to see if I can hit a bull elk in the neck while he is on the run and I'd like to try it."

Steve says, "Get yourself a good rest on that tree and I'll goose them when you are ready."

Jose says, "I'm ready."

Steve stood up, waved his hat and yelled. You know what happened. All those elk took off for parts unknown. The five-point went angling down the ridge. Ker-Powie! Over he rolled. When they got over to the elk, Steve said his head was folded back under him. He straightened it out and Jose had broken that bull's neck with one shot offhand. No rest.

While they were dressing out the bull, Jose told Steve he had won the gold in rifle shooting the year before at the Olympics and also many awards at Camp Perry, the National Rifle Association shooting facility. This was true. It was the year that the Mexican team wiped out all contenders for the gold in the world Olympics.

Camp at Big Prairie.

AN INCOMPLETE EDUCATION

When a guy hears of a wreck, automatically he sees a truck and a car or a car that missed a turn or something like that. Now the wrecks I write about now are real and all done with mules and horses, all caused by who knows what.

In hiring a crew you try to find men who possess certain qualities. The man you want has to be aggressive, have ingenuity, be of a gentle nature, be a quick learner and above all be able to use practical knowledge. Many college degrees are given to people who have no practical knowledge. Carl had no practical knowledge.

A string of mules is tied together with pigtails. A pigtail is a small rope secure to the cinch on each side of the pack saddle running up through the back D on the decker and lays out in a loop on the mules hips. The lead rope of each mule is tied to this loop so it will break if a mule stumbles or blows up and the whole string won't go down. It doesn't always work, as Carl proved.

I was in bad need of a packer one year—just had more parties than help. Now you just don't step out and find a man who knows mules, packing and how to deal with people and have a good all-around personality. I called my friend Smokie, who runs a top outfitting school. "Smoke, you got any boys that I can depend on to drag the kitchen string?"

Smoke says, "Yeah, you call and talk to Carl. He'll do you a good job."

Carl shows up and away we go up the trail. I'm ahead with the guests, Carl following with 10 head of mules and the camp. We stop for lunch but Carl doesn't catch up. I jump on my horse and lope down the trail to see if he is having any trouble. Well, I round a turn at the bend in the river where the trail comes around a rocky cutbank. There's Carl standing, looking at his mules all in a pile. He'd jerked them off the trail by taking the curve too fast. Some were upside down, some standing with packs under their bellies, some flat on their backs. I rode right up behind Carl and stopped. Carl is talking to himself; he doesn't know I'm there. He says, "Damn that Smokie! I took his school three times and he never once told me this could happen."

When the trip was ended and Carl had had no end of trouble, he came to see me and asked for time off to go to town. I says, "Carl what you got to go to town for? I need help packing firewood and you just came from town."

Well, Carl, in his funny way, says, "If you don't mind, I'd like to go and seek other employment."

I says, "Pick up your check at the house and I'll get by some way."

That wasn't the end of it. Steve needed to tow an antique car to town so it looked like an opportunity to kill two birds with one stone. Well, Carl wrecked the pickup and car on the way to town. In the short time he'd been with us, he cost us better than $800 besides his wages. In seeking other employment, he gave us the better part of the deal.

Donna Copenhaver and several Pennsylvania hunters with their trophies.

THE MAN FROM SPAIN

One day I got a call from Jack Atcheson, a hunting consultant, and he explained that he had these fellows from Spain who wanted to hunt bull elk and he wanted me to take them on a hunt. This was along in the middle of November and we were planning on pulling our camp as the season was about over. It was the last hunt of the season. We made the necessary arrangements and were all set to go.

Now these two gentlemen were to hunt antelope for three days and then I'd pick them up in Missoula and we'd go to elk camp. One was General Franco's son and the other, Paco, his cousin. As it turned out, only Paco came. Paco was a 6 foot 4 inch man of 260 pounds of nothing but soft flesh and fat, just as awkward as a cow with a broken leg. He said his partner was short, fat and lazy. "He no good," was Paco's words. I only smiled and wondered about Paco.

When we got home from Missoula, I had a phone call that one doctor who was to join us would be a day late. So Steve and the other boys left for camp next morning and I waited for Jack, the doctor, to arrive. I told Steve he'd better guide Paco and just give him an easy day. I would be in the next day and take Paco under my wing.

When Jack and I arrived at camp, Steve and Paco were already in camp. Steve said he couldn't get Paco out of sight of the horses. Steve took Jack out the next morning and I took Paco. I went up Dwight Creek which was to be a very easy hunt, not a lot of steep climbing. I planned to hike up a game trail to the head of a little creek where we could set and glass a large area. It was bachelor haven for bulls after the rut. We had made it about halfway when Paco gave out and said, "We sit." So sit we did in a little open snowslide area. We were eating lunch when out of the corner of my eye I caught this bull moving up the side of the mountain through the lodgepole timber. I showed him to Paco and said, "Take a rest over this stump and when he comes out above that thicket and on the open hillside, aim high on his shoulder and let him have it."

When the bull came out and I could see him, I knew what we had. It was the "Dwight Creek Bull." This old boy had lived here for seven or eight years, many times shot at, but seemed to have a charmed life. He was huge as elk go and always sported a large six-point rack with extremely long, ivory-tipped points. His royals were extra long, a trophy in any man's land.

Right here I must tell you about this old bull. He was big, old and smart. He knew all the tricks of evading a hunter and always seemed to have the big advantage in pulling the disappearing act. Some guides say you have 10 seconds to shoot a bull. Well, this old boy didn't have a watch...

He always ranged the Dwight Creek country with his harem and when the rut was over he'd pick up a couple of young bulls and travel with them. He really liked Danaher Mountain. Him and his two pals would feed the open hills at night and when they went to bed for the day, he would pull off to the side where he could watch the younger bulls from his bed. If a hunter spooked the young bulls, he'd be gone off the other way, always giving the guides the slip. Sometimes the hunter would get a shot, but it was always a miss.

He also had a very distinct track on his right hind foot. The outside toe was an inch and a half shorter than the other, leaving a very pronounced track any guide would remember once he saw it in soft dirt or snow.

He became a legend and a challenge to all my guides as well as to my son, Steve, and myself. As Steve puts it, "It ain't no fun hunting Dwight Creek any more without that Old Bull."

Now Paco misses three times 'til the bull is out of range. We set and watched him amble up and around the mountain. I says to Paco, "Let's to after him. I know just where he is going and we can get him easy."

He says, " Me no climb mountain," and I could not get him to go any place but back to camp.

I told him, "Now if you won't go, I'm going to take Jack in the morning and get that old boy."

He says, "Me no climb in the snow." So Steve was stuck with him next day.

Now Jack had hunted elk for 14 years and had never gotten close enough to any to even look at them through his scope. He was one of the Helena Wilderness Riders and the summer before I had told him either Steve or I would get him a shot at a bull if he'd come the last hunt while we were pulling camp.

Well, we took off early next morning and climbed up a snowslide to where I thought this old bull would feed that night and, sure enough, his tracks were there. I circled to find out where he went to bed down at. We followed his tracks very slowly through the timber for a couple of hundred yards. He had followed a big game trail, making it easy for us to follow him. We had about a foot of soft dry snow, real quiet going, just what we needed. Suddenly, I saw his orange rump patch. He was bedded about 60 yards ahead. I stopped and showed it to Jack, but before he could raise his gun, Mr. Bull stood up and stood broadside to us. What a beautiful animal! He was huge and with a sagging backline that comes with age. Jack wasted no time. One shot and he had his bull. As we stood admiring that trophy, Jack says, "You don't know it, but today is my birthday and a better present I could never get." As I remember, he would have scored over 400 in Boone and Crockett, the official international scorers of trophy animals.

Oh, yes, for Christmas I received a package. In it was the foot of the Dwight Creek Bull. Jack had had an ash tray made for me. I just love it. Thank you, Jack.

Now I was back to Paco. As I said before, he had hunted mule deer and antelope in eastern Montana before he came to me. His outfitter had said he was a good shot and had killed both antelope and a buck at extreme ranges with one shot each. Now shooting at that bull he was sure sloppy, so Steve took his rifle out and sighted it in. It was 16 inches off in elevation and about two feet to the left. It was a fixed scope and we could do nothing about it. Jack gave him his rifle and a box of shells and showed him how to load the gun.

We took off up Whiskey Ridge. I had a place in mind where these old bulls hide out after the rut. The trouble was we'd have to climb high through knee-deep, soft snow and come into this pocket from the east or the wind would take our scent right to any game in that area. I tried every way I could to get Paco to move a little faster and climb steady. Finally, I just told him how worthless he was and a disgrace to his country. This made him mad and he really got with it and up the mountain we went. I had used this tactic before and it has worked, but you had better show some game or you've lost the ball game.

We finally reached the top of the ridge and I sat down and gave him a rest while we ate a sandwich. I glassed this basin and found where these bulls had been feeding the night before. I explained to Paco how I plann-ed to hunt it and that I'd done it before and was sure we'd be successful if we could walk quiet enough. A storm was coming in from the west and this would help us a lot with the wind in the trees and snow falliing. We should be able to walk right up on one of those bulls. By this time Paco was elated. He had never realized he could climb so well. In fact, I think he was very proud of himself, especially when he could look down so far from where we had started.

I picked the largest track and started to pussy-foot one step at a time as we were in heavy timber and had poor visibility due to snow coming down hard. We had gone only 200 feet into the timber when I spotted this pair of antlers sticking up over a log. I threw up my glasses and there lay a nice six-point bull, sort of above the log. There was snow all over his body, making it hard to see him at first.

I finally got Paco zeroed in on it and told him, "Now shoot him in the chest cavity." Paco lets go a shot and out of his bed came this bull. I said, "Shoot again."

Paco says, "I have no bullets."

Me to him, "Where they at?"

"In my pockeet," he says.

I dig in his coat pocket and stuck a single in his rifle and says, "Shoot." All this time the bull is flopping and running straight to us. Bang! Paco does it and down goes the bull. There never was a happier Spaniard, or a guide, I might add. Success can heal a lot of wounds. The bull was shot right cross-ways through the hams three feet from his shoulders. Paco was still a poor but lucky hunter. Next day we all went to get Paco's elk off the mountain—sort of had a party doing it.

We packed out the next morning and when we got home my wife, Marg, says, "I found a buffalo for Paco." Now before we went to elk camp, Paco had insisted we get him a buffalo.

I says, "Paco, I'll have to buy a buffalo from some rancher who raises them and you'll just ride a wagon around in the bunch 'til you see the bull he wants to sell. Then we'll throw out a bale of hay and you'll shoot him."

He says, "Fine. In Spain the man who has the bison, he is the big."

So the next morning early we are at Gehring's ranch out of Helena and, with a wagon drawn by a John Deere tractor, we are hunting buffalo in a small fenced in pasture alongside of the state highway. Paco shoots the buffalo and we take some pictures for him. While the boys are caping the head for a mount and skinning the rest for a rug, I jump in the car and head for the airport as Paco has a 2:30 flight, one leg back to Madrid, Spain.

Now for the whole story. Paco arrived in New York from Spain on the 12th of November, flew to Billiings, Montana, where he spent two days hunting antelope and mulies. The outfitter, a friend of mine, drove him to Missoula that night. I picked him up and took him hunting the 16th of November and he got a six-point bull. We were back at the Helena airport by 2:30 o'clock November 23rd and he was on his way to Madrid, Spain, from New York the morning of November 24th.

This gave Paco 12 days from Madrid back to Madrid and he had lucked out with one six-point bull elk, a four-point mulie, a 14-inch antelope and a buffalo. Every animal was shot even though he couldn't shoot straight—known as "beginner's luck."

GENTLEMAN
F R O M GERMANY

Not many years ago I booked a gentleman and his wife from Germany. Now Horst was 6 foot 1 inch or so and Rosemarie a little redheaded gal.

Rosemarie was the dean of women at the University of Mannheim, Germany, and Horst was a Doctor of Agriculture. He owned some big farms in the Ruhr Valley, some of the most fertile farm land in the world. He was about 70 years old and straight as a pool cue, very military. During World War II he was the field marshal over the troops and big guns along the French Coast. In our conversation he said he hated Hitler and was an avid admirer of Ike Eisenhower. I asked him why he was Hitler's field marshal if he disliked him so much. In broken English he says, "Me not field marshal, me get," and he drew his finger across his throat.

This was a special hunt. Me guiding and Horst hunting, Rosemarie observing, and my brother-in-law, Joe, cooking.

Each country has its own ritual that is followed very closely when hunting big game. Austrians I have had worn a kind of leather skirt or britches and carried a round, green sort of tablecloth made of felt. They would spread it out on the ground and then would come up with a bottle of schnapps and some silver shot glasses. The guide and guest must drink a toast to the game before eating lunch. Horst and Rosemarie were no different. They followed rituals also. Bedtime was one of them.

Our camp was composed of two 10 X 12 wall tents facing each other with a kitchen and dining area in between. We could drop the flaps on the sleeping tents and you'd actually have three rooms, so's to speak. Rosemarie would never drop the flaps when she put Horst to bed. She would stand there and as Horst shed one garment at a time, she would fold it neatly and place it on a stand beside his bed and give him his pajamas a piece at a time. When he had crawled into his sleeping bag, she would come to the cookstove with a turkish towel, warm and fold it just right and then go in and wrap it around Horst's neck and shoulders, place the sleeping bag cover up under his chin, pat him on the chest and give him a little peck kiss on the forehead, turn around and prepare herself for bed. When she was all tucked in she would holler to me to come in and put out the gas light. These things are just not done in our American way of life. When Mother Nature called on them, they just stopped and relieved themselves. No thought of exposure. This was their custom. Everyone has to go, so what!

Horst carried a single-shot German Mauser, 7 X 65 Mag, and a special staff that folded out at the top to make a beautiful rest for shooting. The first morning we were leaving camp on foot. It was still dark. We had only gone a few steps when Horst says, "Howad, one moment please." I stopped. He and Rosemarie came up to me, Horst thumbing through a little German and English dictionary and Rosemarie holding a tiny flashlight on the pages. He mumbled to himself a little bit, then his face lit up with a big smile and he says, *"Howad, wememba dat de fun of de 'unt is de 'unting,"* closed his book and away we went.

When we left the cook tent, Joe stuffed our lunches in a backpack. I put it on but noticed Rosemarie reach for it and I said, "I'll carry it." The farther we went that morning the more sullen she became. I couldn't figure her out. Finally, I thought mebby she wants her packsack for some reason. I took it off and offered it to her. Her face lit up in a big smile and she says, "Woman's job take care of manz." Now everybody was happy.

We were going up a steep hillside with lots of rock. I wanted to drop into an alpine basin where I knew there was a good bull. We came out on an open hillside and, "bang," a bull bugled right across the draw from us. He sure caught me with my pants down. We could do nothing but lay down in the rocks. Finally, after much sweat, this bull worked his harem over the ridge to the west. We had to wait 'til all the herd was out of sight or we'd spook them.

As soon as I thought we were in the clear, we headed after them, climbed a rocky ravine where you should never ask a hunter to go, but they were game and we made it. We climbed the ridge and settled beneath a big fir tree and I gave a bugle, expecting the bull to be on the far side of the canyon by now. Back he came with his answer about 100 yards below us. Now came the fun. I'd bugle, he'd answer, and then we'd try again. The suspense was terrible. Rosemarie was almost uncontrollable; old Horst was as calm as a cucumber. All of a sudden here came the bull right to us. He stopped about 25 yards from us, bugled and raked a tree with his antlers. He just kept it up. You could not get Horst to shoot. He just sat, aiming with his rifle. Finally, a breeze of air hit me on the neck and away exploded our game. Needless to say, I was perturbed. I says, "Why didn't you shoot? That was as nice a six-point bull as you'll ever get."

In his broken German accent he explained that a real hunter would only shoot such a magnificent animal if he could place the bullet in the flank behind the front leg, assuring a heart shot, and this bull only faced us. "I could not see der spot." Well, we went to camp happy, ready to try another day.

When we came to the foot of the mountain and were walking up the horse trail to camp, I noticed Horst was sort of limping along. When we got to camp he immediately pulled his shoes off and was looking inside of them. I says, "Horst, do your shoes hurt your feet?"

He says, "Yah. I buy dem in a sporting goods store in Italy last summer.

Der no goot." I looked at them and handed one to Joe. These shoes are beautiful leather but fully lined with goose down. Now Horst's feet had sweat terrible that day and the down lining in the shoes was wet. All of the down was rolled up in little balls. Joe and I tore out the lining and the soles, made some felt insoles, and dried the shoes by the cook stove. The next morning away we went again. That evening when we arrived back at camp Joe says to Horst, "How did the shoes work today?"

"Very goot and nice," says Horst. "How you tink the Italian can make goot shoes when he eats only spaghetti?"

The elk were in full rut and there were no other hunters in this area at that time. I got him up on nine bulls in 12 days and could not give him a good look at their flank. So no shooting. Finally, one morning we got in between two bulls that were bugling their heads off. We'd slipped up a draw from below and they were one on each side of a tag alder thicket. I got Horst ready and gave a toot on my bugle. Back came a bugle from my left and a bit above. I bugled again and now both bulls were hot and heavy on the horn. All of a sudden through the tag alder I saw this big bull coming. I say, "Be ready, Horst," and pointed at the spot.

With a crash of brush and a bound, out of that tag alder brush came a small-racked bull. He looked like he was scared to death. Two big bulls were bugling, one on either side of me and right in front of him! He stopped, then jumped up on a high rise of ground, stepped forward with his right leg and "Ker-Boom" Horst had a bull elk.

As I have said, in most foreign countries sportsmen have a strict ritual that they follow after a trophy is taken— and also some when hunting. I've had men from Austria, Switzerland, Germany, Spain and Mexico. They all do it. It seems us North Americans are in too big a hurry to put up with it.

When this bull hit the ground, Rosemarie ran up to him, breaking off a sprig of a huckleberry bush. She stuck this twig in the wound, got blood all over it, and ran back to Horst, who was just standing there; she put the twig to his lips, then blew her breath on it until it was dry and stuck it in the sweatband on his hat. Then we went to the bull where Horst gave the honor to the magnificent bull by taking off his hat and saying a few words in German.

Then he says to me, "Howard, you take the tongue first." I did, and then dressed the rest of the bull.

Now when we got to camp he said to Joe, "You cook dis whole, don't cut." So Joe threw it in a pot and boiled it. When it was done we all had to have a thin slice. Then he threw the rest out for the birds. "You must put something back," he said and that ended it.

Horst and Rosemarie would hunt and fish Alaska with Linn Castle. The following year, Horst suffered a massive heart attack while fishing with Linn and passed away a few months later. A finer gentleman I have never met.

Fording the South Fork at White River.

Packing out a bull elk on the Red Hills in the Dry Fork.

THE COMEDIAN

In my years in grizzly country I have had a lot of association with these old boys. I think they are the number one animal in the woods. They've chased me, kept me in a tree all day, torn my camps up, stole my elk and deer, and entertained me. I love the grizzly. He is smart, clever, fast, deadly when he chooses, and, beyond all, unpredictable— the greatest animal in the woods.

In search of food he is not choosy. He loves anything he can get in his mouth—ants, grass, berries, elk, deer, sheep, cows, whistlers (marmots), or people groceries left in camp. In search of these, his ingenuity is unbelievable.

One time while guiding a guest I heard this noise in a thicket off to our left. When I went to investigate, I heard the muffled sound of a bear running away. There was a big spring running out of the hillside where game watered. When I got there, here was a large mule deer buck laying dead. There was deer hair hanging from the branches of trees all around up to 15 feet high in the air. Now this bear had laid in wait and when the buck came to drink he had slapped him with his mighty paw, felling him as if the buck had swallowed a stick of dynamite.

I've seen the grizzly in search of a marmot, digging under a rock with half his body hid in the hole and throwing dirt out between his hind legs like a big badger. Also, I've seen him standing with his ear to a rotten log, listening for ants or termites in the log.

A friend of mine photographed two grizzlies, one on each side of the river, running an elk down the stream until the elk fell, exhausted. Then they walked in, drug it to the shore and had their lunch.

I've seen them run and play, rolling and tumbling like little puppy dogs.

Now sheep and cattle are easy pickings for him and once in a while he will help himself, developing a hatred from the ranchers concerned.

He also loves food in people camps, especially anything in a can or wrapped in paper.

The grizzly leaves behind him a trail, making him the most controversial animal on the North American continent. I admire, respect and love him.

I had a guest hunting grizzly up in the Mission Range one year. This range of mountains rises between the Seeley-Swan Valley and the Flathead Indian Reservation on the Flathead River. They form an extremely high, rugged spine of granite peaks topped with glaciers year around, a most spectacular sight, high, rough and rugged—perfect grizzly country.

It was hot and dry in late September. We stopped to eat a sandwich right on top of Panoramic Peak one day. This is right on the Flathead Indian Reservation line.

While we were eating we heard this noise like an old cow bawling over on the northwest side of McDonald Peak. It just kept up getting louder and sometimes it sounded like a man yelling for help. I says, "Doc, let's hang our packs and rifles on this tree and go have a look." We cut across to where we could look down into McDonald Lake on the Indian side. There is a big glacier running up the side of McDonald Peak.

Climbing up the edge of the glacier is a grizzly bear. He is bawling his head off. When he gets to the upper edge of the glacier he stops and sits down like an old man in an easy chair. He'd sit there, waving his head around, and beller and bawl, and then sort of lean back in a sitting-up position and down the glacier he'd go like a kid on a tobaggan. Now, when he came to the edge of the glacier and rocks, he'd rock up on all fours and up the hill he'd come for another slide. To sit there and watch an animal weighing from 600 to 800 pounds hollering and playing like a kid on a snowslide made you wonder who is king—man or beast. We watched him for a while, kicking ourselves for leaving our cameras in the packsacks.

I never told anyone about this for a long time. I know they'd think I was lying. Then one day my friend Andy Russell from Canada told almost the same story in his book *Grizzly Country.* So the Mission Mountain grizzlies are not the only ones that should be in the world Olympics.

SHIMA

I rode into hunting camp one evening and was greeted by one of our guides. "God, am I glad to see you! We've got this joker who no one can get along with and all he wants is a bear. You've got to guide him 'cause we won't."

I says, "Now it can't be that bad. You don't know how to handle him."

I unsaddled my horse and unpacked my mule. I'd been in the Bob Marshall Wilderness on a three-week grizzly hunt with another client. This elk camp was up in the Bitterroot Mountains right on the Idaho-Montana state line, a very productive elk, moose and deer area. I went to eat supper and I guess the word got around. Into the cook tent came this Japanese doctor. With no introduction or anything, he says, "Can you show me a bear? All I want is one shot and I'll be happy. My daughter, Amy, wants a bear rug."

I says, "We'll see what we can do tomorrow. What kind of rifle do you shoot?" Right then the flavor of the conversation changed.

"I have a 338 caliber Winchester model 70." This rifle had just come out. It is tops in getting elk, moose or bear of any kind. I told him what a smart choice he'd made on his first rifle. You see, he had never hunted western game before. Said he'd hunted whitetail a couple of times. Before I had finished my last cup of coffee, Doc and I set up a lasting friendship. We both fit each other.

Away we went the next morning, on foot. I asked him how tough he was and he said he was tough enough to go wherever I did. Now I was in good shape and young, mebby 40 years old and Doc was a bit younger. After a hard day and no luck, I dropped down a creek drainage where there were lots of wild blackberries and raspberries. Now if you haven't walked through blackberry vines, down timber and rocks, I'll tell you it will sure pull the salt out of a man. I notice Doc is having a hard time keeping up so I sat down for a rest. When we started out again I says, "Doc, let me carry your gun for a ways. It's tough going through this rocky gorge. I'll stay right in front of you and if we see anything I'll hand you your gun."

He says, "Fine."

Well, now we had gone just a short way when I spotted a big ole brown bear fast alseep on the upturned root of a big log. I took my time and we slipped right up on him, real close, mebby 50 yards. I says in a whisper,

"Look at that big log, Doc. Right at the butt end is your bear, fast asleep," and gave him his gun.

Well Doc lines up on him and misses him slick and clean. The ole bear stands up, stretches and yawns. Doc lets go again. Another miss. Mr. Bruin stops again, looks us over and starts up the log. Now after another miss Mr. Bear puts it in overdrive and disappears.

I says, "Doc, where were you aiming?" He says, "Well, at the distance and speed he was traveling I led him about four feet and elevated about four inches." Me, I shake my head and asked him if he knew how fast his bullet is traveling. He says, "Yes, 3,000 feet per second."

I asked, "At what range are you sighted in at?"

He says, "Dead on at 250 yards."

I asked, "Do you have a piece of paper and pen in your day pack?"

"Yes," says Doc.

I says, "Get it out. I want to show you why you missed your bear."

Now Doc is a very well educated man and smart as a whip. He says, "OK, what shall I write on this paper?"

I says, "I personally have clocked a bull elk at top speed on flat ground and all he could go was 35 miles per hour. That bear was going up hill and not running. You should be able to figure this out. Say he was 100 yards away and you're sighted in at 250 yards and you raised your point of aim four inches, where would you hit him? Also, we'll say he was running at 36 miles per hour and your rifle shoots at 3,000 feet per second and you led him two inches, where would you hit?" We sat and I smoked a couple of cigarettes. All of a sudden Doc starts to laugh and says, "How dumb can I be? I'd miss him a mile any way you go." We both had a good laugh and a good hunt and went home to supper in a fine mood.

The next day Doc got a real nice six-point bull elk and there were no misses and no windage or leading.

The last night in camp Doc says to me, "If you were going after a grizzly, what color would you want?"

I said, "I'd want a bald-faced, full silver-tip. There are as many different color phases in grizzly as a lady has in her closet on the rack."

He says, "OK. How about you and me hunting until we find what you would like? We'll take nothing but full silver and bald-face if it takes 21 days for the next 10 years."

I says, "OK, we'll start the hunt October 15th next fall."

He says, "Fine." And that's how this story begins.

There was never a word ever said about the $100 deal, but come Christmas I had a Model 700-338 Winchester for a Christmas present. Doc was a very generous gentleman.

Come October 15th the next year and we're on the trail to the back country. We were headed into the Scapegoat Wilderness Area to a spot called Cooney Creek where I had a cabin rented from the Forest Service. This cabin was an old line camp for some sheepmen up 'til about 1926 or

27. It was very rundown but we had reroofed it and put a floor, doors and windows in it. It was one of our main camps for hunting elk and deer. This country was and still is some of the best grizzly country in Montana.

After a couple of unfruitful days of hunting, we woke up to a real old-fashioned blizzard—snow, cold, wet and really sour weather. One day we came in early. The snow was about two feet deep and still coming down with a northeast wind. We were sitting around the cook stove with our feet in the oven trying to dry out our cold feet. We were all facing the window behind the stove. I was facing Jim, the cook, when the funniest look came on his face. I turned to the window, looked out in the storm and if Mae West had been standing out there I couldn't have been more surprised. A huge black bear was coming right at the window. Jim hands Doc his rifle and I opened the window. Doc stuck his rifle out the window and Amy had her bear rug. He was huge, had a long coat of jet black fur, as fine a trophy as one could want.

We hunted hard after the storm slowed up, saw bear and tracks, but no full silver-tip. Had to give it up and wait for another year, but Doc went home with a fine bear rug for his daughter and a good billy goat.

The next year we decided to hunt the Mission Mountains along the Indian reservation. Now the Mission Range is a very high and spectacular backbone of mountains that divide the Swan Valley from the Flathead Valley. The western side of this range is the Flathead Indian Reservation, so non-Indian people can only hunt to the divide line on top above the eastern and northern side. This is very good grizzly and goat country. The only trouble is that it depends on the season. If you have a good huckleberry crop on one side or the other, the bear will be on that side of the mountains. This year I speak of the berries were heavy on the Indian side so our luck was no good.

Someplace in this book you will read about the Panoramic Grizzly. That episode happened on this hunt.

Well, another fruitless hunt, so we set down and planned our next year's hunt. Just me and Doc are going. We will do a lot of backpack work out of a very movable camp. This sets just right with me because I like to hunt 'til I find a bear I think might be the one I'm looking for and then, with a small pack and a few candy bars and a ground cover, just live with that bear 'til you get a look-see at him. Doc was game and a better partner you could never find.

We were to hunt the head of Little Salmon River just over the Smith Creek Pass in the roughest part of the Swan Range, a beautiful piece of high, rugged mountain if there is such a thing. Here you have Tango Basin, Cataract Gorge, the Big Burn on Palisades and Owl Mountain, along with Stadium Peak and three big creeks or basins at timberline. But, my friend, you got to be tough to hunt this country. It surely cuts the boy out of the men in a day or two.

One evening about 5:30 I spotted five grizzly feeding on a big slide on the north side of Tango Mountain. We were about seven miles away on the south face of Owl Mountain. As the sun broke through the clouds, I could see the face of this one bear and through my binoculars I could tell this was our bear.

After Doc and I had studied them for a while, we decided to get our horses and ride up Little Salmon trail to a spot about two and a half miles from the bear and then take it on foot as close as we could before dark. We'd find us a spot to hole up for the night and go after them the next morning.

Doc sat down to rest and I started looking for a suitable place to spend the night. We were right up against the base of the cliffs that formed the top rim of this big basin above the Smith Creek Lakes.

All of a sudden I noticed a pile of rocks like the Indians used to mark their trails. I followed it to where it joined a goat trail up and along the base of the cliff. The trail made a turn into a crevice on the cliff and to my surprise there is a cave back in to the cliff. It was about 30 feet long and 10 to 12 feet deep with a rocked up fireplace, very crude but the circulation of the air carried all of the smoke out and up the side of the cliff.

The floor of the cave was covered with old alpine fir boughs about two feet deep. All of the needles had fallen off many years ago. The branches had a black mold or fungus on them that showed extreme age. We dug them up and sorted through the needles and dirt on the floor, looking for something that would determine the age of previous use. We found rabbit skulls and chicken feathers and one leg bone I guessed was a front shin-bone of a deer. Whoever had lived in this spot was a woodsman of high intelligence. We cut some fir boughs for a bed, made us a fire and rolled in for the night.

I have questioned all the old-timers of the area and none knew about this cave. There is an old Indian trail that crosses the divide out of the South Fork coming into the Swan Valley that passes not far below this spot. In my mind, I think it was either Indians or an early-day mountain man's camp. One thing for sure, Doc and I surely enjoyed his hospitality even if we were uninvited.

During the night a storm came in, as happens in high mountains at this time of year. The next morning it was snowing and blowing 'til you couldn't see three feet. I says, "Doc, if this is like most of these early storms, it will blow out by noon and we can find their tracks because if there is anything grizzly like, it is to feed when the weather is rough. They've got their winter underwear right with them and it make the marmots and squirrels sleepy and lazy, easy to catch. Grizzly feed on rodents they find in rockslides at this time of the year."

Along about 11:30 the wind would blow the clouds out of the basin for a few minutes. Then some more would drift back in. Finally, about 1:00 or 1:30, we had patches of blue sky and some sunshine. It was beautiful with the fresh snow on everything.

I says, "Doc, let's go." We took off in the direction of the slide where we'd last seen the grizzlies the night before. When we rounded a big spruce thicket, right in front of us out in the middle of the slide were four grizzly and Old Baldface right in the middle. How to get to them was another question. If I went to the right, the west wind would blow our scent right to them. If I went left, we would be out of sight of them. Long ago I learned never to lose sight of a grizzly or you will lose him. There was only one way, straight up the rock slide, keeping rocks between us and the bear. It was a tough stalk on our bellies and hands and knees most of the time. Finally we rounded a big boulder and the bear were about 150 yards off, above us. I tells Doc, "Now we'll slide under the upper side of this boulder and you take a good rest and be sure to break his front shoulder. No matter what happens, stay flat, keep shooting and don't say a word. I'll cover you if it gets too rough." Now, only a couple of fools will shoot a grizzly uphill above them when that old boy has his buddies with him. But this was four years and no grizzly and here was the one we were looking for.

Doc shoots and that bear let a bawl out of him you could hear a mile, and down the slide straight at us he comes, dragging one leg. Doc had pulled off and gutshot him. I whispered "Let him have it again." He shoots and more of the same, dead center but in the wrong end. Now, a bear rolling and bouncing downhill isn't the best target. Also, all three of

Prime grizzly country in the Bob Marshall. Lots of high and rocky cirques.

the other bear were running along with him, bawling and raising cain. Finally, the last shot got the right spot and stopped the bear. Now we were in trouble. If we showed ourselves, we'd have three mad grizzlies right on top of us so we had but one choice, stay under the rock and see how much cold we could stand.

The dead bear lay there 75 yards from us and sitting on top were three mad bears. They would set on him just like a man would. Every little bit one of them would jump up, run around and smell the air, run back to the dead bear, and then another one would make a circle bawling and sniffing the air. I finally figured out what we had. We had a family, an old sow and three yearling cubs. They kept us pinned under that rock 'til about 5:30. The old sow finally stood up and took off around the slide. She'd come to a big rock, sniff it and roll it over. The yearlings would dive in and feast on any squirrel or whistler asleep under it. Some rocks were as big as a grand piano and she rolled them over with ease with one paw. Such power in an animal of 400 to 500 pounds was unbelievable.

Doc and I skinned the bear and headed for our horses. It was dark by now and we were sure cold. Doc's bear was just what we wanted. We had our trophy on the seventh day on a 21-day hunt and four years of tramping the woods.

When we got to the horses I couldn't get close to them. I'd been carrying the pelt and must have smelled like a bear to them. Doc finally got on his horse and I had him ride up to mine and untie him. Say I, "Doc, you lead him and I'll walk and carry the hide." So down the trail we went to camp seven miles away. I'd stop and rest every once in while and lay the bear hide in the snow. We finally made it to camp. I took care of the horses and mules and then went in to get some supper. Doc had the fire going in the stove and the coffee pot was boiling, but Doc was fast asleep on his sleeping bag. I opened some soup and pork and beans, and made some toast on top of the stove. I hollered, "Come and get it, Doc."

Sleepily he says, "Get it yourself," and fell back to sleep.

The next morning we broke camp and packed the mules. I rode out in the lead with Doc following. All of a sudden I stopped. I couldn't believe my eyes. There in the snow was a trail of bear tracks making a circle around our camp. They had followed our tracks off the mountain, smelling the blood trail where the bear hide had dragged in the snow. I say, "Come here, Doc."

He rode up beside me and looked at the bear tracks. We sat there, not saying a word. All of a sudden he says, "We got what we came for. Let's get the hell out of here before they get what they came for." And we did.

I hope Doc reads this wherever he's at. He is the greatest.

TUNNEL VISION

One evening I get a call from my son, Steve. He says, "I've got this guy from California who wants to book a hunt for him and his wife. The wife doesn't want to hunt. She wants to go along and enjoy camp life while John does his hunting. John wants a really good bull and you will have her around camp all the time." (I'm doing the cooking.) "There is one problem," Steve continues. "John has very poor eyes due to an accident. He calls it tunnel vision. He can only see straight ahead and when it gets dark he can't see anything."

"Well, you've got a problem. This is going to be tough," I says.

Steve says, "You've guided hunters in worse shape. At least this guy can walk in daylight."

I says, "That's right, I guess. Anyway, you're the boss and you'll be guiding him."

He comes back, "Well, I've already booked him."

John told Steve his problem was sort of like looking through a pipe. It takes time to get focused on an object, somewhat like comparing a side angle binocular with an old-time telescope. You see only a small circle in front of your eyes.

When John and Mary arrived, Steve brought them into camp. I was already there with two hunters and their guides. Mary and I hit it off well. She was used to camp life and fit right in.

Steve and John hunted long and hard. Steve is a guy who believes as long as you can see you hunt and you can always get back to camp no matter how dark it is. He doesn't make a regular habit of coming in after dark, but the times he has it has paid big dividends for him and his hunters. Well, Steve would get on a bull, but by the time he would get John's eyes focused on him, the bull would take a powder and be gone. A guest like this always seems to really be long on determination and guts. It also gives a guide a subconscious desire to try harder and make sure his guest gets every chance he can give him.

It was getting late in the hunt and Tim and Dan had gone home. There was just John and his wife, Mary, Steve and I left in camp. Steve says this morning, "I'm going up the center ridge in the Dry Fork. I know it's tough and John has trouble seeing his footing, but I know that old herd bull is still in there with his cows somewhere. Maybe I can spot him across a canyon someplace and have time to get John to see him before we jump him."

This is rough country, rocky, steep and with deep canyons with open sidehills every once in a while. It really is not a country for someone with bum eyes. Steve and John rode as far as they could to save John a rough climb, and then took off on foot.

They hunted out several basins, seeing nothing but tracks and a few mule deer. Finally, Steve told John to sit and watch and he'd climb a high rocky ridge and look into the last big basin of this creek. When Steve started to glass this basin from the top of the ridge, he spotted a cow down and across the basin, then another, and a calf or so. Finally he spots a bull and a spike on the high side of where the cows were feeding. This is a beautiful basin rimmed by red cliffs on three sides with strip timber running all the way down to the Dry Fork. Real elk country.

By now it is getting late, around 4 o'clock in the late fall afternoon. He hurries back to John and tells him, "I think we can get to the bull if we hurry before it's too dark to shoot. But then we'll have to drop down to the main trail and have nine miles to walk before I can climb up and get our horses. Then we'll have another four miles to ride to camp. What do you say? Shall we try it?"

John thought for a moment and said, "That's what we came for, isn't it?"

Steve says, "Let's go."

When they topped the ridge, across from them and below they could see 11 head of elk feeding up a meadow coming in their direction, only a mile away. Steve found a ravine with loose dirt and gravel that he and John could slide down into the basin. They got into a finger of timber and hustled down into the basin, coming out above the snowslide the elk were feeding in. At the edge of this opening is a huge rock mebby 20 feet high and 30 or 40 feet wide. I've sat on it and glassed many a time.

They stepped up on this rock and right below about 300 yards were the cows and calves. No sign of the bulls. All of a sudden, out of some brush about 200 yards came this old cow in a big hurry with the spike right behind her. He planned on starting a family of his own. With a bugle and bawl, right behind him came the old herd bull shagging him off and regrouping his cows. John got that old telescope lined on a shoulder and "Bango," he had his bull.

Now comes the pay-off. You always have to pay for good things. It's now about 5:30 and they're losing light. Steve dressed out the bull and John and him headed for the main trail. Steve says, "Give me your gun and you travel as fast as you can."

When they reached the trail it was dark as the inside of a cow. Steve cut him two canes and said, "You keep right against me and I'll tell you when a rock, log or rough spot is in the trail."

They walked along this way for a while and finally John says, "I just can't see a thing."

Steve says, "It's full moon tonight. Let's sit down and wait for the moon to shine into this canyon."

That they did. Along about 9:30 the moon peeked over the high ridge on their left. It was really light, almost like day. John did fine until he'd hit the shadows of the trees; then he couldn't see. He'd put his hand on Steve's back and they'd shuffle along 'til they hit light again. When they reached the lower end of the Dry Fork, Steve built a fire and climbed back up the center ridge and got their saddle horses.

Now me, I'm trying to keep supper warm and console a wife who knows she'll never see her dear John again. She's sure the grizzlies have them or they have fallen off the edge of the world. Finally, she cried herself to sleep about midnight so I went to bed.

I was rudely aroused at 3:30 the next morning by Steve and John. They wouldn't stand still for a cold, warmed-up supper. I had to cook them fried potatoes and steak, but I was really glad to cook a fresh supper for a man who would buck the tiger so hard and come out on the big end of the stick. Needless to say, Mary, dry-eyed and bouncy, had to eat with them.

The next day she and I went along with them to get the bull and we really had a nice time. The weather was perfect. It was a beautiful ride—a perfect climax to what she believed was a tragedy.

Steve Copenhaver with the Dwight Creek bull.

SOMETIMES YOU CAN'T WIN

For five years we hunted the upper Bitterroot country right on the Idaho line. This is a big area of high ridges with heavy timber on the north and east slopes and grassy, open hillsides on the south and west exposures.

Jack, one of my guides, was not having very good luck in getting his hunter a shot at a good bull elk. He was an inexperienced hunter and Jack dug deep into his bag of tricks. It is sometimes necessary in this guiding buisness to do things that look foolish to your hunter but are necessary for a successful hunt. But sometimes nothing works.

Well, Jack spotted two nice bulls bedded down out on an open hillside. He showed them to his hunter and explained, "We will go around and get in that timbered draw, then sneak up to the edge and I'm sure you can get a shot before they spot us. Bull elk are smart and you just don't walk up on them too easy."

Well, when Jack and hunter got up the timbered draw to about the right place to take a look-see, Jack motioned to his guest, who was right behind him, to get down on his knees and follow him. Jack makes like a coyote on all fours and slips along up out of the draw very slowly as to give his guest plenty of time and looking ahead to make sure he does not spook the bulls by showing himself. Every few seconds he'd hear this buzz, buzz behind him. Concentrating on the sneak and the bulls, he paid no mind. Jack stuck his head up over the edge of the bank and the bulls were laying there looking right past him.

Jack glanced off to the side and there was his hunter, gun slung over his shoulder and taking pictures of Jack with a movie camera as Jack made the sneak. Jack exploded, "What the hell are you doing? What do you think I'm doing down here on my knees?"

The hunter says, "I don't know but I wanted some pictures of you tracking elk." You can guess what happened to the elk. They exploded into thin air and so did Jack.

Another year we were camped on Warm Springs Creek. This was a big, open country with big, grassy hillsides with strip timber and a timbered pocket here and there, making excellent elk hunting country.

In camp this particular hunt were two guests that hunted with us quite often. They were buddies and always hunted together with one guide.

They were short, fat and dumpy and you couldn't get them to shoot nothing, but they always saw lots of game and had plenty of shooting. I believe they had more fun missing and laughing about it than if they'd got one. While you could really enjoy these boys, no one liked to guide them because you knew they'd miss. Poor old Jack drew this pair.

Now Jack loved to hunt Andrews Creek. It was very heavily timbered, facing into the north and east. The elk would feed on the head of Andrews Creek by day and come over the mountain in the evening to feed the open hills sloping to the south and west. Riding up to Andrews you had to climb a sharp ridge, then drop through a little basin, over another ridge and through another basin. This kind of country continued clear to the top of the divide into Andrews Creek, about four miles of slow traveling. He knew they wouldn't walk so he says, "I'm going to ride up to Andrews Pass every day and wait for evening and hope they'll hit one."

So it went. Every morning Jack, John and Jake would ride to Andrews. Most every evening they would see elk but would foul up some way and miss every time. These old boys knew their weakness very well so they packed two boxes of shells in their saddle bags at all times. We accused them of starting up a sporting goods store on the mountain.

This day I'm speaking of was their last day of hunting on this trip. They left camp in a jubilant mood. Jack was as keyed up as they were. John and Jack seemed to stimulate your frame of mind.

I was high on a mountain to the west of them when I heard them shooting not far above camp. All was silent for 45 minutes or so and then another barrage of shots. This went on all morning. I counted thirty-some shots coming from their side of the basin. I said to my hunter, "Jake and John, one or the other, had to hit something this trip."

He only laughed and said "I'll bet they're shooting at rocks so they won't have to pack all those shells home."

When we got to camp that night Jack was in the cook tent surrounded by all the guests. Now Jack can tell a story well and in telling he does much of his talking by waving his arms and jumping up and down.

He said, "You know that first little basin you drop into from the low ridge? Well when we topped over there was three bulls feeding in it. I got John and Jake off their horses and loaded their guns. The bulls paid us no mind. I had them lay on their bellies and rest their rifles over rocks and they started shooting. Well the bulls trotted over the ridge up the main trail.

"We got on our horses and rode on up the trail for Andrews. When we topped out into the next basin, here them damn bulls were again. So they got to shoot at them again. No luck. Over the next high ridge the elk went on a run. I figured, well, this ends it all. With that much shooting there won't be a grouse left on the hill.

"We loaded up and went up the trail again. When we rode into the big basin, just under the pass there are those same three bulls feeding peacefully. I got Jake and John off their horses and slipped around through the timber and came out right on top of them bullls, not 50 yards off. Jake slipped and rolled down the grassy hillside but John shot at them, again missing."

Like I said, Jack used physical action to tell a story. He's really getting wound up now when "crash," the camp chair he's sitting on breaks and Jack falls to the floor. Without a word someone hands him another chair and he continues. "We rode on up into the pass and I found a protected spot, where I could glass a lot of country, and built a fire. We ate our lunch and waited the afternoon out. I wanted to try that big, open sidehill one more time. Along about 4:30 I explained to my guests that when we got to the top of the ridge I would sneak out and look over and down the sidehill. If elk were there I would wave and they should come to me and make a last try at shooting elk.

"I tied my horse and slipped out to the edge of the hill and peeked over. There were about 40 elk, all spread out feeding. I waved to them to come but couldn't get their attention so I picked up some rocks and hit one of their horses. They looked up and seen me. Here they came, pounding on their horses on a high lope. I jumped up and stopped them, grabbing the first horse. Now John jumps off his horse, runs around behind to get his gun, slips and falls right between the horse's hind legs. As he goes down he grabs the horse's tail. This spooks the hell out of old Chief and down the hill he goes, wide open, straight at the elk. John jumps up and takes after poor old Chief, hollering 'Whoa! Whoa! Bring my gun back.' Away down the mountain goes the elk, followed by Chief and John in high pursuit." No elk, no nothing but a royal hunt.

I had the pleasure of guiding John and Jake's sons in later years, as well as some of their friends. They have told me John and Jake have told of these hunts many times and the enjoyment they gained was worth more than trophies on their walls.

Jack Atcheson with a dandy bull.

INDUSTRY CHANGES

I've seen many changes in my life from Model T's to jet airplanes and sawbucks to deckers. Now we'll talk about outfitters. They have changed also. Very much.

It used to be that you knew the outfitters who were in your immediate area. The others really didn't amount to much, just a bunch of renegades as far as you were concerned. Now this was just because you didn't know them and they were competing with you and using your pet country. You just didn't like this. Most outfitters called it infringement. Me, I call it ignorance.

Right here I am going to jot down some of the history of the outfitters of Montana. Way back in the 1930's, Joe Murphy and I called a meeting of all the outfitters along the west side of the Continental Divide that we knew. We wanted to get them together and start something. Well the meeting place was at Joe's ranch. The people who showed up were Joe Murphy, Fannie Sperry Steele, Chip Dunlap, George Moore, Dick Hickey, the Copenhaver brothers, and Tom Edwards who was just starting into the business. We had a fine get-together and formed an organization called Western Montana Outfitters and Guides. Oh, yes, I left out one man who really gave us help in those years, Elden Myrick, of the U.S. Forest Service. It wasn't much of an organization, but it really grew from then on.

Well, it grew and grew. It didn't happen all at once and we had some pretty hot conventions, but everyone has become a sort of big family now. It has caused each outfitter to improve his services, equipment and business in general. We all could see something someone else was doing that showed us a better way to do ourselves. We have become very friendly and are able to work together in solving our common problems and management with both state and federal agencies such as Forest Service, Fish and Game, U.S. Fish and Wildlife, B.L.M., and also with private landowners.

Finally, some boys from the Gallatin and Livingston area came and wanted to join us. Now this posed a problem. They were from the east side of the Continental Divide.

We had to change our name. We argued all afternoon and couldn't come to a decision in naming the organization. Finally, Old George, the

Getting set up for the ride by adjusting the saddle stirrups, with plenty of help. Photo by Bill Browning.

oldest outfitter, stood up and demanded the floor. In his droll voice, he said, "I'd like to make a motion." In his own words, Old George drolled, "I make a motion that we summer foller the son-of-a-bitch and go to the bar and have a drink." The day's business was adjourned. The next day it was decided to name the organization the Montana Outfitters and Dude Ranchers, as these new fellows operated dude ranches as well as pack outfits. Up to this time it was strictly a back country horse organization.

Then there were a number of associations started all over the state. Outfitting for deer and antelope really increased. We needed unity and numbers for badly-needed legislation. Again, something had to be done, so with everybody getting together we finally formed the Montana Outfitters and Guides Association, taking in the whole state and it is still growing. We now have an organization of North American Outfitters taking in all hunting states as members, giving us a very broad field of ideas and unison in solutions. It has helped to establish laws and regulations that are a must in this day and age.

We have conventions where we can sit down and hash problems over on a very mutual ground. It used to be I might want something from an agency and my outfitter friend over the hill something else, contradicting each other's efforts to gain a little bit that would help the industry. In all, it has upgraded the business to where we have some unity in services that a guest can rely on as well as with the agencies we work with. We have helped each other upgrade our own outfitters due to pride and necessity if we are to survive in this competitive business world. I say "thanks" to the efforts of a lot of good men for many of the changes. Some changes have been good, some bad, but together we can win.

The outfitters were the first conservationists in the state. We had to be to protect our future and our pride. I'm sure this will continue with the new young brains that are in the lead today. It surely is a different kind of ball game today than it was back in the good ole days.

Now we'll go to game—elk, deer, black and also grizzly bear. I have seen the rise and fall of game numbers in this Bob Marshall and Scapegoat area, along with the Bitterroot Range, several times.

I have seen the elk when there were too many for the winter range—winter kill due to starvation 'til you couldn't stand the smell some places when you passed them on a summer trip. I remember one employee of the Forest Service who picked up a quart jar full of elk ivory teeth while opening the trail in the spring from the Danaher to Big Prairie in the Bob. The teeth I speak of are small ivory tusks that grow from the upper jaw right in front of the molars. As the elk grows older and the teeth wear down they are stained a beautiful chocolate brown with light rings forming the shape of a moccasin on the exposed top end. These are used as sets in lots of western jewelry. The Indians used them as buttons and decorations on their buckskin clothes.

Before this winter kill, for several years right in the middle of hunting season I've seen the Danaher Valley when you couldn't tell where one herd of elk ended and another began. There also were lots of mule deer. We'll never see this again in my life-time even if the hunting season was closed for several years. What made the difference was the big forest fires we used to have. Mebby someday again, but it takes about four or five years for the vegetation to set up after a big fire and another four or five years for the elk to increase. But I'm afraid us humans won't let it happen as nature would will it. We've got to interfere.

We had lots of mountain goat not too many years ago, but due to the slowness of any control on hunting licenses they've gone way down in numbers. I've seen hunters packing out nannies and kids with spikes 2 1/2 to 3 inches long. This only happened because a hunter could buy a goat tag for an additional $5 bill just to be able to say, "Yes, I've shot a mountain goat." Thank God that is something in the past, but it will take years for them to increase anywhere like they used to be because they are extremely slow reproducers.

Now fishing is another big item with me. This back country of ours has some of the finest fishing in the world. In years past it has been misused terribly due to people catching too many fish. It should be a catch and release area. We now have a strict limit in the wilderness area, but we had it once before and people got it changed through the legislature. I hope we can hold it this time. I really believe we will. It seems to me most sportsmen are far more concerned about what they are leaving for the next guy than they were a few years ago. To show you what I mean, I have seen piles of cutthroat trout thrown away because fishermen saved every fish they caught. Others set up canneries along the rivers. I have not seen this in the later years. All I can say is, let's all hope it is a permanent trend.

> The Redman's Cow is vanishing now
> And so is the Grizzly Bear.
> The Elk and the Moose and Canadian Goose
> In numbers he's still fair.
> The Rainbow and Browns
> Have taken the streams
> That once were the Grayling's dream.
> I hope there's a Cutthroat Trout
> Somewhere about
> When my great grandson fishes these streams.

AN AVERAGE HUNT

So you want to know just what goes on on an average hunt.

The most successful hunts are a one-on-one hunt with time being a major factor. I have kept a day-to-day diary off and on over the years just to see for myself how hunts go. Following is a typical hunt:

September 14th. There are five hunters, five guides and myself as chief biscuit burner and one packer on this trip. About 8 o'clock we're at the corrals saddling and packing mules. Today is one of those nice days with a cold, drizzly rain lasting all day. The sun just won't come out. Steve, the boss, has hurt his back so can't make this trip. At the doc's. Sure going to miss him. Arrive at camp about 3:30, get all situated for camp life and a good supper.

September 15th. Breakfast over and all hunters gone by daylight and I might say right here that they never returned for supper before 9 to 10 o'clock any night this trip. These boys hunted hard, long and in adverse weather conditions. Due to lots of rain the game hit heavy timber and stayed there. Today the guides had 19 different bulls bugling. Never saw anything but cows and calves and two mulie bucks.

September 16th. I'm using guide's names to designate who saw or got what. Todd called in a bull, hunter couldn't get a sight on him. Dan and Dave saw bulls but couldn't get anything done. Tim and hunter saw cows and calves, got a bugle.

September 17th. Tim's luck was no good again today. Todd's hunter passed up small bull. Dave's hunter passed up good mulie, no elk. Dan saw bull but no luck.

September 18th. Dan's hunter got five-point bull. Tim saw nothing but had bugles. Dave saw plenty of deer. Sid saw deer, one buck, fair. Todd's man missed five-point bull.

September 19th. Dave saw 11 cows and three bulls, no luck. Todd still bugling them on Lake Mountain. Tim still sees only deer. Sid's hunter got five-point bull. Dan and hunter packed out bull killed yesterday.

September 20th. Dan, Sid and hunters went to pack out Sid's bull. Dave's hunter got six-point bull. Tim still no luck. Todd saw bucks.

September 21st. Dan and Sid's hunters each shot two nice bucks. Todd's hunter passed on five-point bull. Tim saw cows, calves and deer. Dan and Sid's hunters packed out six-point bull.

September 22nd. Tim still tough lucking it, no bull, but had two bulls bugling. Todd got hunter large mulie buck.

September 24th. Everyone saddled, packed and headed for home this morning. Must have hit the trail by 10 o'clock. What do you know, the sun is shining today.

Let's do a little analyzing to see if this was a successful hunt or not. In all there were three bull elk and three mule deer bucks taken by five hunters. This don't look so good, but add the rest of it up.

There were five takeable bulls passed up by hunters hoping for a larger one and two good bulls missed under 100 yards.

There were three trophy bucks taken and every hunter had a chance at at least one buck.

From my standpoint it was a very successful hunt, but to the hunter who went home without his bull elk, mebby it looks different. I'm sure I don't know. I guess a guy just has to look at this bit of statistics and make up his own mind if its a good hunt or poor one.

Now to show you what part Lady Luck has in hunting, our man Tim is one of the top guides in the business. He's always been tops in getting game over many years. He came back next hunt and came in with the No. One bull the first day. So you might just as well admit we're all only as good as the Good Lord makes us.

An elk that is both old and big.

CLOSE QUARTERS

In September of 1948, me and my two brothers, Gene and Wendell, guided a party of six hunters from Cleveland, Ohio, into the mountains 30 miles from our home ranch on the Big Blackfoot, in western Montana. We were out for elk in the Bob Marshall Wilderness Area. We camped on Danaher Creek, at the head of the South Fork of the Flathead in prime game country. Snow had come early. The ground was patched with three or four inches, enough for tracking, and the prospects looked rosy.

Late the second afternoon one of the hunters killed a nice bull on Hay Creek, about two and a half miles above camp. It was decided that I would have the job of bringing the carcass home to camp the next morning. At daylight I saddled my horse and started out in the direction of the kill, leading two pack horses—a full-grown elk is too much for one. I didn't want to leave meat lying in the woods any longer than I could help on account of bears. An elk or deer left overnight is likely to be half eaten by morning.

The bears are more plentiful some years than others. That fall was a bad one for the beasts; they were hungrier than usual. The berry crop had failed and every bear in the mountains was on the prowl day and night hunting for anything that would fill an empty belly. So I wasn't surprised to see bear sign several times as I rode up along the creek.

Half an hour from camp I encountered a jackpine thicket that was too much for the horses, so I tied them and went ahead on foot to find the elk and pick a trail for the horses up to it. I hadn't walked far when I crossed another fresh bear track, and the farther I went the more sign I saw. I began to think that if I found the elk in one piece I would be lucky. I started to hurry then, impatient to run off any bear and salvage what remained of the meat. But I was too late. When I got to the place where the bull had been dressed out I found only a few leavings and a broad, tell-tale trail where a bear had dragged the carcass.

I was mad. What guide wouldn't be if he had outfitted a party of guests, herded them a hard day's ride back into the mountains with all their supplies and gear on pack animals, set up camp and spotted his hunters in first-class game country, only to have a thieving bear lug off the first kill? I had blood in my eye and just one idea in mind—to get back what was left of the elk and do it right away. And at the same time, I would teach the bear a good lesson.

I had hunted all my life and outfitted and guided for over 20 years. With that much hunting experience I should have taken a second look at the bear tracks before doing anything else. But in my anger I overlooked that little detail. The sign I had seen farther down the creek had been made by a black bear, and I took for granted this was one of the same breed. I knew it was big, for the elk would have dressed close to 400 pounds, but it didn't cross my mind that the bear might be a grizzly.

The trail was easy to follow. The bear had taken the elk up and around the side of the mountain, and it had made easy work of the carcass considering its weight. After 300 yards the track dropped into a series of deep washes and then angled up a steep slope toward an isolated stand of thick spruce. I knew I was getting warm. No bear would take an elk through there. The bear had headed for that thicket on purpose, seeking a good spot to stop and cash in on its night's work. I would find the bear in there somewhere, with what was left of the loot—which probably wouldn't be enough to pack out. I was getting madder by the minute.

I stopped at the edge of the timber and went down on one knee for a look-see. It didn't take long to find what I was looking for. I saw a patch of dark fur move behind a log, 25 feet up the hill, and then I made out the outline of an ear and saw an eye staring in my direction. The bear had seen me first.

The rifle I was carrying was light for the job. One day many years before, as a boy, I had shot a box of 8mm. shells at a coyote, which had been about 1,000 yards off. I hadn't killed the coyote. My shoulder had taken a pretty severe lacing, and as a result of that incident, I had developed the bad habit of flinching when firing any gun that slammed back at me. I had never been able to get over it, consequently I stayed away from the wallop packers. Most of the time I toted a .25-35 Winchester saddle gun.

I know it sounds screwy for a man in my business, but I prefer that little gun and do better with it. I knew a .25-35 really wasn't rifle enough for a big bear, even a black; however, I figured if I put the treatment in at the butt of an ear I wouldn't have any trouble. The ear was conveniently exposed over the log, and I was close enough that I couldn't miss. As I brought the rifle up, slow and easy, the bear came up too, fast and hard. It reared on its hind legs and let go a deafening roar that was enough to knock my hat off.

That roar told me, a little late, that I wasn't dealing with a black. I had walked into a grizzly as short-tempered as a stick of dynamite, and all of a sudden the little .25-35 seemed hardly more adequate than an airgun.

We looked each other over for mebby 10 seconds, although to me it seemed like a quarter of an hour. I noted that the bear was a handsome old sorehead, with a dark, silver-tipped coat that shone like frost, even in the dim light under the spruces. I held the gun on the bear and waited for it to make the next move, hoping it wouldn't be in my direction. When the grizzly didn't move, I took a cautious step back, and then another. I kept backing up until I had a reasonable amount of yardage between him and the timber. The bear stayed put. I dropped down into one of the washes and then got out of there fast. I didn't intend to lead the pack horses back to camp unloaded, but I knew I would have to kill the bear if I wanted to claim the elk.

I decided to come in from above and try for a shot in the open, at something more than 25 feet away. I made a big circle and worked warily down the hillside to the upper edge of the spruce thicket. I thought I knew exactly where I would find the bear. It would be on the elk or beside it, waiting. But I had figured wrong.

I was down on one knee again, trying to see under the branches, when the silver-tip cut loose with another roar so close behind me that I thought it must be looking over my shoulder. I spun around and stared the bear in

Grizzly trail, in the snow, across the Danaher Meadows. Photo by Bill Browning.

the face. It was just six yards off.

It wasn't a pleasant sight. The grizzly was up on his hind feet like a man, eyes blazing, lips curled back and emitting a rumbling growl, the hair on its neck and shoulders all standing the wrong way. It looked 20 feet tall, and scared the hell out of me.

I had no chance of stopping the bear at that distance with the .25-35, and I knew it. No matter where I hit it, the bear would keep coming until it got me. There was only one thing to do; find a tree and, and if I could reach one in time, climb. A grizzly can't follow a man up a tree.

It was a slim chance. There was just one tree of the right size anywhere near, and it was between me and the bear. When the hunters paced it the next afternoon, they found I had been 10 feet from the tree, the grizzly eight. I didn't have time to think. I must have acted from instinct, or from something I had learned in the Navy—that a surprise offense is often the best defense. I yelled in the bear's face and jumped for the tree.

My yell must have startled the grizzly for a second or two as much as the bear's roar had startled me, and my head-long rush kept it off balance just long enough. I was already in the tree when the grizzly started for me and out of reach when it arrived.

When I started my dash I had had my rifle with me, but when I reached a safe perch about 20 feet off the ground, I missed it. Looking down, I saw the rifle laying two or three feet from the base of the tree; the bear was smelling and cuffing at it. I realized later that no man could climb at the rate I had to and hang on to a rifle.

The grizzly blew its cork over my getaway. It danced around under me, bawling and raging and clawing bark, tearing up the ground like a baited bull. I was high enough in the tree to see the elk carcass in the spruce thicket, about 20 yards away, and I kept hoping the fresh meat would lure the bear off. Finally it did. The grizzly turned and lumbered down the hill, stopping every few steps to throw a warning growl back. When it reached the elk, it lay down beside the carcass. The bear, however, kept its head turned toward me.

The first thing I wanted to do was to get my rifle. I gave the bear a quarter of an hour to settle down and get interested again in the elk. Then, I started inching toward the ground, lowering myself from one branch to another.

I was careful to make no noise; the bear paid no attention until I was almost down. Then suddenly it seemed to sense what was going on. It lurched to its feet with a bawl of pure hate and came streaking up the hill. A bear can really cover ground for a short distance when it wants to. I went back up the tree a lot faster than I had slid down. The bear tramped around again under me for a while, grumbling and snarling, but finally made up its mind it couldn't reach me and went back to the elk.

I gave the grizzly time to lose interest once more, and then I tried another cat-footed descent. The same thing happened. The grizzly let me get down to the lowest branches; then it bounced up and came raging for me.

It's hard to believe, but the man and the bear kept that up for more than seven hours, from half past 8:00 in the morning until almost 4:00 in the afternoon. I lost track of how many times I went up and down the tree, but by late afternoon I was worn to a frazzle and realized that I couldn't keep at it much longer. Unless I succeeded in getting the rifle on the next try, I would have to give it up. And that would mean sitting in the tree and waiting for help to come from camp, a prospect I didn't relish. Gene and Wendell wouldn't start to look for me until dark, and I kept thinking how they would probably blunder into the grizzly then. I wanted to prevent that. But how?

Unexpectedly, however, the bear's attitude changed. It must have been getting just as tired of chasing me as I was getting tired of climbing. Or mebby it merely became resigned to the situation—it couldn't catch me in the tree, and I wasn't going to risk coming down on the ground. As I started down for my final try, the grizzly, lying on the elk, was growling and blustering and balefully watching me. When I reached the lowest branches, the grizzly stood up and bawled its resentment. But it seemed unwilling to be tricked into making any more runs up the hill, unless there was a fair chance of getting a crack at me. That gave me the opportunity I had been waiting for all day. When I had reached a point about my own height from the ground, I braced myself, legs tense and ready for a fast ascent. Cautiously I broke off a forked branch, reached out with it and raked the rifle up. I felt almost secure as I started back up the tree with the weapon in one hand.

But even before I was back on my perch, I knew I wasn't going to risk using my pea-shooter on the grizzly, after all. There was only the slimmest possibility that I could kill it with one shot, once it was hit and went off into the thick spruce, I wouldn't have a second chance. There was still Wendell and Gene to think about. If they came up along the creek after dark, hunting for me, the bear would be formidable enough. Wounded, it would be almost certain to kill one or both of them. Somehow I had to get out of this fix myself, while it was still daylight.

During the day, I had looked the hillside over countless times, but now I took another look and thought I saw a way of escape. As near as I could figure, it was about 60 feet down the hill to the elk carcass, where the bear was lying. Thirty feet the other way, up the hill, there was another tree I could climb. Beyond that one was a third and a fourth, each a little farther apart. If I could make it to the first and then on to the others, by a series of dashes and climbs, mebbe I could finally put enough distance between me and the grizzly so that the bear would stay with the elk and forget about me.

The first lap would be risky, but it was the only way to keep Gene and Wendell out of trouble. I would have 30 feet to cover while the bear was coming 90 feet. If I could get a running start, I figured I could make it.

I let myself down to the lowest branches. The grizzly watched every move I made, growling ominously. It took all the nerve I had to let go and drop to the ground. But once I was sure the bear wasn't going to get up before I hit the ground, I did it. I lit running. I heard a gruff bawl as the grizzly lumbered to its feet, and could hear it pounding up the hill in pursuit, but my 20-yard start was too much for the bear. I was safely up the second tree before the bear got there, and I had even managed to get my rifle up in the tree with me.

The bear was snorting and tearing around at the foot of the tree; then, after a few minutes, it gave up and went back to the elk. The next tree was about 50 feet farther up the hill. As soon as things quieted down, I dropped and went for it. It was duck soup this time. The silver-tip again came charging after me, but it had too far to run now to cause me any real concern. It took four trees, nevertheless, and a total gain of 75 yards before the bear called quits. It chased me up those four, one after the other. When I came down from the fourth tree, the bear paid no attention.

To make sure, I backed away a few yards, one step at a time. When I saw that the bear stayed put, I took off up the hill, watching it over my shoulder. I made a wide circle to get back to the horses, and then I started for camp.

It was dark when I rode in. I had expected my long absence to have caused some anxiety, but nobody showed any. Somewhat to my annoyance, my story provoked more amusement than sympathy. It took me a couple of hours to convince my brothers and the rest of the party that I wasn't just spinning a tall yarn. It was hard for them to believe that a bear would keep a man in a tree for a whole day. They finally were convinced that I wasn't kidding. Before turning in, the party had everything arranged for settling the grizzly's hash the first thing the next morning.

"If he's still there," somebody put in.

"He'll be there," I predicted grimly. "He won't move 10 yards as long as there's a mouthful of that elk left. If we want him, we'll have to run him out."

The six hunters and three guides left camp at sunrise, following Hay Creek for a couple of miles and then riding straight up the mountain to get around the bear. I remembered an open ridge that gave a clear view of the creek bottom, the hillside and the spruce thicket. We planned to post the hunters along that ridge. Then Gene, Wendell and I would move down on the grizzly and flush it out. By following this plan there was no way for the grizzly to catch us with our pants down, as it had caught me the morning before. It was a good plan and it would have worked, except for one thing we hadn't figured on. Nobody needed to go into the brush and flush that grizzly out. It was ready to come out without any prodding.

After tying the horses a safe distance back in the timber, we moved down to the ridge on foot. Most horses will bolt at even grizzly sign in a trail. We knew we would be asking for a big package of trouble if we tried to take them anywhere near the bear. We were bunched on the ridge 300 yards from the thicket, getting ready to send the hunters to their places. The bear was nowhere in sight. Then all of a sudden we heard a commotion on the hill below.

"Here he comes!" Gene yelled.

The grizzly had boiled out of the thicket and was plowing up the hill at a dead run, apparently hell-bent on tackling all nine of us. We let the bear come 30 or 40 yards, waiting to see if it really intended to go through with it. Then, pulling up and standing on a fallen log, the grizzly reared high on its hind legs for a better look. We didn't wait any longer to see what the bear would do next, but we all agreed afterward that it would have kept coming if we hadn't killed it. The grizzly acted every bit as reckless and vindictive in the face of nine-to-one odds as it had the day before when it had put a lone man without a gun up a tree and kept him there for nearly eight hours.

Gene got in the first shot. He belted the bear in the shoulder with a 180-grain Core-lokt from his .30-06, and the grizzly dropped off the log with a bellow that shook the ground. But it didn't go down. It whipped around, bit at its shoulder, pulled itself together and came pelting up the hill again, straight at us.

Then the mountain fell in on the bear! We were yelling and shooting and the horses were rearing and plunging. Three or four good solid hits were scored.

The bear kept its footing through the whole barrage, but seemed to be aware that it was licked. Still roaring defiance, it wheeled and started the other way as Wendell spiked it in the back of the head with a softnose. The grizzly was less than 100 yards from us when it went down.

When we skinned the bear we found it had copped nine hits, of which any one, given a little time, would have been fatal. The grizzly, however, had stayed on its feet until that final shot which had blown its brains apart. A bear that's aroused enough to attack man can absorb an amazing amount of lead.

"I was glad I hadn't tried for him with the .25-35 the day before!" I confessed when it was all over.

We went back later to look over the sign and piece together how the bear had managed to surprise me the day before. It had come out of the thicket on the downhill side, picked up my tracks and trailed me as a hound trails a rabbit, following me while I circled to get above the thicket. It had stalked me with the stealth of a cat. The snow was frozen and crunchy, yet the grizzly had crept up to within 18 feet of me—we paced the distance between my tracks and the bear's, and even measured it with a steel tape—without a whisper of a sound. Then it had stood up and bawled, ready for the final rush. Some hunters say an unwounded bear won't stalk a man, but that one certainly did.

Howard Copenhaver with his 25-35 carbine and the grizzly that gave him the run.

The pelt squared nine feet, as beautiful a silver-tip skin as any of us had ever seen. They estimated its weight at not less than 800 pounds. Some of the eastern hunters, who had hunted Alaskan browns, thought the grizzly would go better than that. Whatever the bear weighed, it's a safe bet that no meaner a grizzly ever roamed the mountains of Montana.

Now as the old Latin saying goes: *Montani semper liberi* —Mountaineers are always free."

BOOKS AVAILABLE FROM STONEYDALE PRESS

THEY LEFT THEIR TRACKS
– Recollections of 60 Years as an Outfitter in the Bob Marshall Wilderness –
By Howard Copenhaver   **Hardcover – $18.95   Softcover – $13.95**

WESTERN HUNTING GUIDE
– A Complete Where-To-Go & How-To-Do-It Guide to Western Hunting –
By Mike Lapinski   **Hardcover – $17.95   Softcover – $12.95**

RADICAL ELK HUNTING STRATEGIES
– Secrets of Calling Elk in Close –
By Mike Lapinski   **Hardcover – $17.95   Softcover – $12.95**

BUGLING FOR ELK
– A Complete Guide to Early-Season Elk Hunting –
By Dwight Schuh   **Hardcover – $17.95   Softcover – $12.95**

HUNTING OPEN-COUNTRY MULE DEER
By Dwight Schuh   **Hardcover – $17.95   Softcover – $12.95**

OREGON HUNTING GUIDE
By John A. Johnson   **Hardcover – $17.95   Softcover – $12.95**

MONTANA HUNTING GUIDE
By Dale A. Burk   **Hardcover – $17.95   Softcover – $12.95**

ELK HUNTING IN THE NORTHERN ROCKIES
By Ed Wolff   **Hardcover – $17.95   Softcover – $12.95**

TAKING BIG BUCKS
– Solving the Whitetail Riddle –
By Ed Wolff   **Hardcover – $17.95   Softcover – $12.95**

MONTANA FISHING
By Dale A. Burk   **Softcover – $5.95**

SUCCESSFUL BIG GAME HUNTING
– Secrets of a Big Game Hunter/Guide –
By Duncan Gilchrist   **Hardcover – $17.95   Softcover – $12.95**

MONTANA: LAND OF GIANT RAMS
By Duncan Gilchrist   **Softcover – $19.95**

ALL ABOUT BEARS
By Duncan Gilchrist   **Softcover – $13.95**

BALANCED BOWHUNTING
By Dave Holt   **Softcover – $14.95**

COOKING FOR YOUR HUNTER
By Miriam L. Jones   **Softcover, ring binding – $12.95**

Ordering Information:

Toll-Free Number 1-800-735-7006

STONEYDALE PRESS PUBLISHING CO.
205 Main Street • Drawer B • Stevensville, Montana 59870